bad dyke

allison moon

Lunatic Ink

Cover and chapter title font is Lemonade by Rachel Lauren Design

ISBN 978-0-9838309-7-9
Library of Congress Control Number: 2014915243

Learn more:
Lunaticink.com

Contact the Author:
info@lunaticink.com

Printed in the United States of America

you know who you are

-A

contents

the skinny

IF THERE'S A clean body of water around, I want to be naked in it. Unfortunately, growing up in Northern Ohio, the term "clean" had to be taken with a grain of rust.

Nevertheless, Lakeshore Park was a regular summer destination. Lake Erie wasn't as bad in the 90s as it had been when its tributaries caught fire thirty years prior. In fact, the water seemed incapable of conducting chemical fires at all anymore.

The summer of '99 was also the summer I came swinging out of the closet. I had graduated out of my dreadfully conservative high school and immediately made my way to the big city. The Big City, in this case, being Cleveland. I joined the LGBT Center and started going to their weekly teenage meet-up groups. The group was mostly boys in ill-fitting pleather pants and a few girls weighed down with rainbow jewelry. But being a queer kid among others for the first time, it all felt like magic.

One auspicious evening we drove to meet some other queer

kids at the park: two girls and one boy. Both girls caught my eye. One was a small white girl with short blond hair, a little rough around the edges, and with the same rural Ohio accent shared by all my cousins. She had a butch, working class scrappiness that was both familiar and hot. She introduced herself as Jo and her friend as Tania.

Tania was a tall, athletic black girl. Her head was shaved, her lips were pillowy, and her skin was dark. I blushed in the face of her beauty. Tania barely spoke, but when she smiled at me, I fell hard.

When our two groups came together, we engaged in the familiar but awkward moment of claiming our crushes. This ritual happened with silent glances, smiles, and subtle attempts to stand near each other. Tania and I claimed each other. Jo also claimed me, but soon realized that I only had eyes for Tania.

The sun was beginning to set over the lake when Jo suggested we go swimming. Some of us tittered the usual "We don't have swimsuits" line. Jo walked to the rocky shore and stripped off her t-shirt and Dickies, revealing a sports bra and boxer briefs. "This works, don't it?" she shouted.

Tania and I shared a glance. I wondered if I was ready to show my nearly-naked body to my new crush before I'd even kissed her. She smiled and shrugged. Then she stripped.

I would like to think I was charmed brazen, but only barely. Enough to follow, if not to strip completely. I unsnapped my cowboy shirt and dropped my denim shorts to my ankles. I waded across the rocks and into the water in my bra and panties.

One of the boys, Daryl, followed after me; he was getting

a perm next week, he said, so he may as well enjoy the water while he could.

The four of us clumped and giggled, waving at our friends on the shore. Tania spied a group of people past the rocks, wading off the sandy beach.

"Wanna make friends?" she asked me, her grin an impossibly-alluring combination of shy and crafty.

Swimming was always where I felt free. I was disarmed. I followed her. Tania did the backstroke, her wide smile pointed skyward. Jo followed. Daryl stayed back. "Uh, guys…?" he said, before his voice faded into our raucous splashing.

I didn't look at the people in the distance, too transfixed with Tania's strong shoulders as she swam. I was one stroke behind her, my fingertips almost reaching her ankle. I timed it so that I would almost touch her with each stroke.

She paused ahead of us to tread water and watch. Jo and I followed suit. The people stood in a semicircle in the water, twenty yards from us, everyone wearing matching t-shirts. I watched, unsure of what was happening.

Jo's eyebrows jumped with the realization. "Baptists!" she hissed.

"What?" I asked.

"Shit!" Tania said. She fled, swimming away as if she spied a shark fin.

Halfway back to our friends on the rocks, we started laughing. Then leaping. Then splashing.

"Baptists!" we shouted. "Three naked dykes just crashed a baptism!"

Our friends on the shore laughed and looked at the semicircle of people now paused in mid-dunk, staring at our weird hair and naked splashing bodies.

Tania and I made a date for the following week. Tania's school friends, a lesbian couple who had been together since freshman year, picked us up in an Astro van with burgundy velour interior. Though they were only seventeen, their relationship seemed cozy and sweet. They seemed decades older when they glanced at us with knowing eyes and jabbed each other in the ribs as Tania grasped my hand. On the way to the movie theater, on the bench seat in the back of the van, Tania and I kissed. Her lips were beyond anything I'd ever felt before, so full and soft. Her lips were like a velvet overstuffed sofa. I wanted to curl up on them and nap. I didn't know that this was what kissing girls could be like. I wanted to kiss her for the rest of the night, just to make up for lost time.

We went to the CedarLee cinema to see *But I'm a Cheerleader*. The boy working the register chided us for missing the first ten minutes, which he said was the best part. We made out the whole time anyway.

After the movie we went to Subway for dinner. We were the only customers. Tania cuddled against me, but I scooted away with a furtive glance to the door. I think I was afraid of being bashed or—more likely for lesbians—harassed and followed.

But the woman behind the counter—a black, middle aged woman in a green visor and apron—smiled sweetly at us. She stole glances over the sneeze guard as Tania curled into my shoulder and leaned up for a kiss. The only bashers were in my own head.

At college I showed all my dorm mates pictures of

Tania, and they cooed. I swelled with pride at the beauty of the woman who let me hold her, as though by merely choosing me, she had assigned me a greater worth.

Tania visited me my sophomore year and we had sex for the first time, our leggy bodies awkwardly navigating my single bed.

When I put my finger inside her, I was shocked at how hot—temperature-wise—she was. It was like putting my finger inside a freshly baked peach. Though I obviously knew what a vulva—my vulva—felt like, experiencing a different person's body, with its unique odor, taste, and feel, made sex a terrifying, thrilling experience.

Tania liked listening to music as she fell asleep, so she put on The Marshall Mathers LP. She drifted off easily as I listened, horrified, to "Stan," the popular track about a stalker who murders his girlfriend. Neat. I couldn't sleep for hours, the quiet flow of lyrics teasing my consciousness awake over and over again.

It was my first small sign that this relationship was doomed.

Our romance continued on and off for another year after that. She would visit me at college and I would visit her over the summers.

The last time she visited, she seemed different. Her shyness led to insecurity. Her outward beauty was invisible to her.

She often mentioned how smart I was and how pretty, always with a pitiable tone in her voice. She stayed silent around my college friends, later telling me that she was stupid and had nothing to add to the conversation. I tried to bolster her confidence, to tell her I thought she was sharp and smart and—jesus, she could go to any college she wanted. She was the one in the private girl's school, with the athletic departments lining up to claim her as their own. She was the one who made my heart stop whenever she smiled.

When I told her how gorgeous she was, she wouldn't blush and bat it away like she used to. Instead, she cast her eyes downward and shook her head, as though I was foolishly placating her.

One night during one of Tania's visits, some friends gathered in a circle to smoke weed before heading out to campus parties. The marijuana, which Tania smoked copiously, only led her further into her own head.

"I don't want to go out," she said. "Stay in bed. We'll blaze and watch dumb movies."

I tried bargaining with her, but she didn't want to go out, meet anyone, feel ashamed of herself. I left her at my house alone and returned at 3 a.m. to find her watching whatever was on network TV at that hour.

Purple smoke billowed from the TV room. "It's 4:20 somewhere," she said. Her sullenness cut the last thread that held me to her.

I went to bed and she joined me later. We slept without touching. The next day she went back to Cleveland, and that was it.

A few months later, she sent me a letter—neat all-capital ballpoint pen on pink stationary. It was a letter I only understood years later when I found it again. She said she liked me and just wanted to kick it every once in a while. She didn't want to put any yokes on me.

The problem was—and still is—I didn't do attraction half-way. I'm either all-in or not interested. And the surest way to douse whatever flame I have is to deny that you're worth it.

I believed Tania when she said she liked me and wanted to keep things casual but fun. I also believed her when she said she wasn't beautiful, or smart, or worthy of my affections. Or at least I believed that she believed it, and that was enough for me.

headline news

THE REC ROOM at the LGBT Center was a concrete basement with folding tables and a few second-hand couches. It was where I learned a line dance called the "Cleveland Shuffle" and where fellow queer teens bitched about their parents, either overprotective or nonexistent.

One evening, as Luis tried hitting the high note in "Oh Happy Day" from *Sister Act 2*, a reporter from The Cleveland Plain Dealer, the city's largest newspaper, came to the Center to do a story on LGBT youth. Journalistically speaking, our group offered plenty of good stories: the butch girl who was kicked out of the house when her father caught her having sex with her girlfriend, the femme boy who switched schools three times to escape bullying and was racing for early graduation so he could move to New York and study dance, the trans girl who grew up in a series of abusive foster families and was working on her GED, and more.

When the reporter asked to take a picture of me and some friends cuddling on the couch in the rec room, I thought nothing of it. Three of the four of us were white and looked well-fed and well-cared for. We were hardly illustrative of the many challenges facing queer teens.

Two weeks later on a humid Sunday morning, my mom called me into the living room. She held up the newspaper.

"What is this?" she asked.

A photo stretched the full width of the page, just below the METRO header. It was the four of us on that couch, legs draped over one another, hard to distinguish one pair from the next. We looked happily engaged in conversation. I was laughing. The headline was "Teens Shun Havens of Sexual Obscurity" and the caption read "Gay teens Allison Moon, 17…" and listed the rest of our names and ages, teasing at the challenges we faced.

Then the phone rang. My mother answered. She assumed her business-woman tone, cordial to whichever concerned citizen was grilling her for details. The phone continued to ring all day. From my bedroom, I got a taste of my mother, spin machine. Most of the callers were the same judgmental suburban moms who showed no compunctions about slut-shaming me when I was dating boys and now feigned concern at the newspaper slandering my good reputation. Through the floor from my bedroom, I heard my mother's placating answers. "You know how kids are at her age," was her preferred canned statement, followed by, "Of course not! She was very much in love with Matt." (Or Chris, depending on which of my high school sweetheart's moms she was talking to).

After hours of damage control, my parents called me into the living room again.

"Why did you do this?" my mother asked, her tone implying this was some sort of spiteful, rehearsed move. Some sort of political statement, maybe. Or one last "fuck you" before I ran away to college.

"How am I supposed to explain this to my colleagues?" she continued, as though my nascent sexual identity would be the most important thing stock brokers would have to talk about on a Monday morning.

They asked me why, when, how, and dozens of other questions which necessitated no answers.

Finally, after twenty minutes of pointless grilling, my father finally asked, "Is it true?"

I shrugged. "I don't know. I don't think I'm *gay* gay. But I like being there. Those kids are way more like me that anyone in school. And I like girls, I think. It's just a thing. It's not some big deal."

Once I got to college, my parents heard only about the boys, one of whom quickly became a boyfriend. Then I confessed to them that I had lost my virginity to my (first) high school sweetheart. These two facts seemed to placate their questions and erase concerns about any nascent lesbianism.

The following summer my grandmother ended up in the hospital, and the family convened as though that could be it for her. We sat—my parents, my father's three siblings, and my assorted cousins, taking up a full corner of the large, powder-scented waiting room.

My aunt helped pass the time by explaining to the assembled family her new bicuriosity.

"I figure why not try it right? I mean men haven't been worth much in the grand scheme, you know? And my friend

Jenny is really hot. So we made a go of it. It was fun!"

My father, uncle, and grandfather squirmed in their Naugahyde chairs.

"What?!" Aunt Carly said. "What's so wrong with two ladies kissing every once in a while?"

My other aunt chewed on her lips.

"I mean really? Everyone's a little bit bi," my aunt pressed, frustrated by the lack of commiseration from her family. "Allison, sweetie!" she nearly shouted. "You are, right?"

This aunt— the baby of my father's siblings, perpetually claiming and reclaiming a party girl mentality while raising a daughter nearly the same age as her granddaughter— grabbed onto me like a life preserver, as she sank into the quagmire of familial disapproval. Instead she dragged me down with her.

I had been minding my own business, consumed by an AARP magazine, when I heard the question. My head shot up, and I found all eighteen Moon family eyes on me.

"What?"

"You're bi!"

My father, who had a penchant for audibly picking at his fingernails, upgraded from snapping to clacking.

"Uh…" I answered. "I…yeah?"

"See?!" My aunt thrust her upward palm in my direction. "There you go," she said, sitting back in her chair, satisfied, as though my existence proved that bisexuality was a family tradition. Far be it from her to let it skip a generation.

My mother and I drove home in silence past the thawing landscape. She tapped her French manicure on the steering wheel, and I watched my breath fog at the window.

"It's normal to find girls attractive and even have crushes on them," my mother ventured. "I did when I was young. Every girl does. But those crushes usually mean that you want to emulate them. It signals ambition."

I squirmed. "Okay mom."

"Interest and curiosity doesn't mean you want to be... intimate...with them."

I stared out the window, hoping to pass a grisly accident that would derail the conversation.

"Do you think romantically about girls? Do you want to...date them?"

I bit my lips, resisting the many thoughts of naked women which now threatened to parade through my head. "Yeah," I said, staring out the window.

"But you like boys so much."

"Yeah."

My mother, her perfect logic failing to sway my identity, sighed and turned on the radio.

A year after that, my parents would meet my second girlfriend, though they assumed she was my first. Hannah was an opera singer—the first of many, for some reason that still eludes me. We drove to my sister's college an hour south of mine to watch a production of *A Streetcar Named Desire.* We joined my parents and my sister and her boyfriend at dinner beforehand. Whenever Hannah would speak, I'd catch my parents sharing clandestine, bemused glances.

Eventually when I came out of the closet once more, as a lesbian, their bemusement devolved into pure bafflement.

On one of their visits to LA, I introduced them to another girlfriend (yes, another opera singer), a small, high-energy woman with pink hair and a tendency to move like an exotic bird in mid-mating dance. I was prepared for the same shrugs and resigned smiles as before. This time though, my mother demonstrated progress in a singularly motherly way: critique.

"I get that you like girls, sweetie. But you can do better. A girl with a little meat on her bones, and a little more between the ears, too."

I pulled into the departures area of LAX, and she continued musing. "I see you with an Eleanor Roosevelt type. Or Susan Sontag or Gloria Steinem. Maybe Ellen! A little more stature. More intellectual heft. Maturity."

I unloaded the bags and reached out for hugs.

My father kissed me and said, "I think she seems perfectly sweet."

"Sweet, yes," my mother said, reaching for a hug. "But my baby needs more than sweet. She deserves greatness."

lucky

ON THE LAST days of my freshman year at college, I felt an itch.

I walked around my dorm in a state of antsy malaise. I couldn't focus on anything. My sleep was fitful and shallow. My moods were erratic, both tears and giddy laughter at the ready. I hadn't yet found a name for the feeling. Instead I described the symptoms to my roommate, a vegan activist with whom I rarely agreed.

"Like I'm cranky, I guess? But energized," I said. "I feel like my brain is an etch-a-sketch that needs to get shook."

"You need to get laid," Janine replied.

I was eighteen. I had had sex with three people, all of whom were "boyfriends," and as such were individuals barely sanctioned by society to allow into my lady garden. I still hadn't had sex with a woman, though the heavy petting my summer girlfriend and I enjoyed indicated that she'd get the garden keys eventually.

My mother taught me that after losing her virginity, a woman is like a bowl of soup that's had dirty fingers dipped in it. I was taught by my woefully incomplete Ohio public school sex education that Abstinence is the Best Choice. But best for whom? And when? Not when I was a sixteen-year-old who was "in love." And not now, when I was ready to rub myself against a tree like a grizzly bear.

It was the week between finals and commencement, which meant the entire campus swam in a sea of hormones. Spring had sprung in a singularly Midwestern fashion, with magnolias and squirrels alike harmonizing "Let's Get It On." No one had an eight a.m. class. No one had a paper to write or test for which to cram. It was a utopia. Two-thousand attractive adults with food and lodging handled, at least for the week, with nothing to do but unwind.

My roommate was getting high and listening to Ani DiFranco with two upperclassmen who were likewise liberated from things like the honey-industrial complex and the virgin/whore dichotomy. Through the open window, a warm breeze carried the scent of a thousand kinds of blooming flowers.

"Here," Janine said, digging through a box beneath her bed. "Use my vibrator."

She pulled out a canvas box and opened it to reveal a purple plastic vibrator crusted with battery acid.

"Uh," I said.

"Damn," Janine said. "It's been a while. Better just find yourself a dick then."

I scoffed. "I'm single." My last breakup was six months prior, and I was still gutted. Though I was a horny eighteen year old, I felt incapable of crushing on anyone new.

"Horniness is like hunger," Janine said. "It's a natural

bodily function that indicates you need something. So go out and find someone to help you out."

"You're lucky," her friend said, peering up from beneath a hand-knit Peruvian wool cap and holding a lighter over the end of the bong. "You're pretty, and you're surrounded by thousands of other pretty people, all of whom are the same age and most of whom are single. This is the best of all possible sex worlds."

I was helpless in the face of her logic but confounded by her frankness. "No, you don't understand. I've just never... done that."

"Sometimes you just need to have sex, Allison," Janine said. "You don't need love. You just need a friendly, willing partner. Go get lucky."

"Lucky," I repeated to myself as I trudged across campus. "What does that even mean?" As though sex were a slot machine. You just had to keep shoving in nickels and pulling a lever until everything came up cherries.

The campus was alight with dozens of parties. I wandered until I heard music, then followed it onto a porch.

At this point I had never been drunk, but something told me my first foray into dick-fishing wasn't a good time to lose my booze-ginity. I sipped on a syrupy cranberry juice and made small talk with other party goers, many of whom I only barely recognized.

I didn't know what a potential casual sex partner should look like, or be like. Everyone until that point I had vetted against a "boyfriend" standard. I didn't need to be nearly so strict, I assumed. I attempted to recalibrate as I refilled my red Solo cup with juice.

Someone had a guitar, and he passed it to a long-haired boy to play. The boy expertly, but modestly, played a few bars and then handed it back. He won me over right there (the giving back part, not the playing.)

His name was Federico Torres, a name he offered with a note of humiliation. Point number two for modesty, though, in retrospect, possible internalized racism. He had a New England intellectual flair, colored by a Brazilian upbringing. He was unassumingly good looking, had a nice smile, and made eye contact when he talked. He wore glasses. We talked about books and travel. I was engaged enough to enjoy myself but not bowled over by desire. He was, I decided in that moment, a terrific fit for a one-night-stand. A perfect practice partner to rid myself of my "sex is an expression of committed love" training wheels.

Federico and I talked for a while, sipping from our plastic cups. It was my idea to leave together. We agreed on his place, though it wasn't really his place, he added. Not promising, but, though my dorm was closer, it also housed three stoned vegans listening to Ani DiFranco, so that wasn't happening.

We stumbled up dark stairs into a dark room and onto a dark mattress in the middle of a bare floor. His thick brown hair fell in my face when we kissed. I tried to brush it away and ended up gripping it in a clump behind his head. Though I would do this with many girls to come, this moment, pre-girls, pre-kink, felt pragmatic more than portentous.

His newness was thrilling and odd. I learned how to kiss him as we kissed. I learned how to touch him as we touched. Everything was the first and only. This kind of sex was like watching a city pass by the window of a train. You see so many things, sometimes things people who live there never see. But it is brief and fleeting and then it's gone.

Sex with Federico didn't last long, but it didn't need to. My itch got scratched.

We drifted off shortly after.

I woke up a few hours later to the heavy morning sun and enjoyed what was to be the first of many strange-room-morning-reveals.

We had spent the night on a mattress on the floor; nothing new for college. What I hadn't noticed until daylight was the white plastic sheeting that draped the walls. White gauze curtains cascaded from the ceiling to form a quasi-headboard canopy type thing. A white stuccoed mannequin sat in parts in the corner. The white-washed hardwood floor was marred by splats of stucco and thick white paint.

Federico slept, his features even sweeter in the new light, his naked body providing the only color in an otherwise colorless room.

I eased off the mattress and found my discarded clothing. As I snapped my bra shut, Federico woke. He reached for his glasses and smiled.

"Good morning," he said.

"Good morning," I replied.

"This isn't my room," he said, as though that would explain the scene.

"Okay," I said.

"My roommates are probably in the living room."

"Okay."

"Thanks," he said. "That was nice."

"Likewise," I said, crawling on the mattress to kiss him

on the cheek.

On the way out I waved awkwardly at the roommates assembled in the living room, smoking weed and gossiping. As the screen door slammed behind me, I heard them cheer "FEDERIIIIICOOOO!!!" On the walk home, I integrated the realization that my mere overnight presence could render a boy a hero to his friends.

Though we never talked again, over the subsequent years I would see Federico every once in a while in a crowded party or across the quad. One party, while cuddled up against a new paramour, I looked across the living-room-cum-dance-floor and saw him politely decline an offered guitar. I thought about how awesome it was to get to have my first no-strings-attached sex with such a simply good dude. I got lucky.

Oh. Lucky. I get it now.

wet and dirty

I WAS A good kid. Didn't drink until college. Got good grades. All the things after school specials tell you to do.

It got me all the things those specials got you: a role as a well-placed extra in the show about the far more interesting kid's life.

Despite the lack of good sense it represents, any good kid will tell you that the role as the good kid only inspires envy of the lives of kids with the gall or shitty home life to entice them to bring moonshine to school in a flask, or get a spring-break abortion after a weekend amateur porn shoot.

Good kids are boring, and we know it.

Not one to try heroin, and enjoying a college education, I rebelled with sex.

I met Eli at a party at his house. He, like many of us, lived in a beautiful Victorian on the edge of town. Having spent my first two years at college as one of the two white girls living in the Spanish House, I learned how to dance salsa right quick. Eli had just gotten back from a semester in Argentina and was eager to practice. We spent the whole party making salsa out of bad hip hop. His room was right off the dance floor, a pocket door that locked with a tiny metallic *chik*.

I climbed on top of him and we kissed, grinding our hips drunkenly against each other like we had more artfully just before.

I unbuttoned his shirt. On his left pec was a new tattoo, an abstract shape. He pointed out the colors to me and their symbolism. I leaned to kiss him and pulled his hips against mine. We fumbled against each other, but he couldn't keep an erection. He cursed that last beer he had, and I said it was okay. We talked for the rest of the night, and I slept happily curled against his side.

The next day, the sky opened up in the year's first summer storm, dashing all plans of getting high on the quad with whichever friends were sticking around for the rest of commencement week. I ran to lunch, splashing through puddles with my Birkenstocks in my hand, and spent the rest of the day packing up my room and reading. My email chirped late in the afternoon. Eli thanked me for a nice night and asked if I had plans for the evening.

He met me on my porch after dinner, wondering if I had an activity preference. I didn't.

"Good," he said. "Grab an extra shirt."

"Uh…"

"Trust me," he said. "Do you want an umbrella?" He gestured to the sky, which had moved from heavy drops to light.

I shook my head.

"Good."

We walked south. The main street led across the quad, past some shops, and quickly into rural houses and cornfields.

Rarely did a student have any business further south than the biggest grocery store, yet I had no impulse to ask until then, "Where exactly are we going?"

Eli smiled and pointed. "There."

I followed his gesture to an aquatic center erected in the middle of muddy field. It was brand new. I hadn't even known it was being built, and suddenly here it was, all new shiny glass, concrete, and blue plastic.

"See that water slide?"

It was a two story tall blue tube standing stark against the featureless Ohio night sky, hard to miss.

"Is this place even open yet?"

"No," Eli said. "The grand opening is tomorrow morning. I've been waiting for a storm like today. It's our chance." Whether or not his logic added up, his boyish grin was impossible to deny.

We ran to the edge of the property bordered on two sides by main streets. The rest of the field backed up on to empty old farmland. The sidewalk was separated from the pool by a hundred yards of deep mud. "Here?" I asked.

"Hell yeah."

We trudged through the former pastureland. The thick, deep mud sucked the shoes off my feet. By the time we reached the fence, mud clung up to my knees, weighing down each step.

The fence was seven feet tall, steel vertical rails and one spanning the top like a giant crib.

Eli bent over and laced his fingers.

"Alleyoop," he said. "Or how about 'Allie up?'"

I tossed my ruined shoes through the fence and stepped

into Eli's palms. He hefted me with such force I nearly overshot the top bar. I grasped it and threw my torso over it, then swung my leg over and perched for a moment. I assembled my bearings and dropped to the cement below in a muddy "splorch."

Eli, the nubile adventurer he was, easily scaled the fence and landed next to me, leaving a pair of matching muddy footprints. He grinned like a beautiful doofus.

"Will it work?" I asked, looking at the waterslide. I didn't want to ruin the mood, but I was skeptical that rainwater would emulate the pump-powered torrent that usually ran a waterslide. He shrugged. "Dunno. Let's find out!"

He stripped naked and ran to the ladder.

I stripped to my underwear and bra, convinced that this rural waterpark hid dozens of state-of-the-art security cameras.

I peeled off as much mud as I could from my feet and eased into the pool. It was cool and perfect, as they often are after a summer storm.

Adjacent to the pool was a natatorium, as brightly lit as a film set.

The banks of white fluorescent tubes combatted the warm orange outdoor lamps, bathing us in starkly shadowed, dawn-like light.

The darkest place was the top of the slide where Eli had disappeared.

He shouted for me to watch. I wanted to shush him, just in case his voice carried the two hundred yards to the nearest structure, a lonely darkened shed surrounded by pine trees. I felt foolish about my fear, but it titillated me. Skinny-dipping was supposed to be dark, in natural bodies of water. Not brightly lit in a swimming pool set to open the next morning.

Eli stood naked on the platform in the sky, then threw himself down the slide. His skin squealed from the friction, but he slid, traversing the fiberglass loops and curves to splash in the pool.

A small rivulet of mud followed him, scraped from his feet as he slid.

He swam over and threw himself on me, pushing my head under the water.

I popped up and splashed him. "Jerk," I giggled.

"Your turn," he said, nodding at the slide.

I climbed the stairs to the platform. At the top, I wrapped my arms around my chest to guard against the chilly night air. To the south was black nothingness, fields leading to fields, separated by single lines of trees. A farm house sat far in the distance, burning a single porch light like a lazy lighthouse.

To the north there was the grocery store, Main Street, and the beginnings of the shops leading toward campus.

Thick clouds covered the moon and stars, and the horizon blended the sky and land in one uninterrupted blur of black.

"Come on!" Eli goaded. "Show me what you got."

I grasped the bar and launched myself down the muddy slide. The fiberglass tugged at my skin. I caught twigs and rocks on the way down, freed from Eli's feet to catch at my flesh.

The lack of water on the waterslide was becoming a detriment to fun. I centered my ass on the slide, using my soaked underwear to provide a bit of lubrication.

I got caught in a loop and pushed myself the rest of the way down.

I splashed into the pool. Eli grabbed me and swept me into his arms. We kissed in the waist high water. There was the possibility of making love right there, except for the lack of condoms. I pushed myself away, smiling, not sure I could trust myself to stop it if we went any further.

"Let's do it together," Eli said.

"I got kind of scraped up on the way down," I replied, showing him the cuts on my elbows and hips.

Eli grabbed his boxers and dipped them in the pool, soaking them. He ran up the stairs, dripping on each step.

"Come on," he said, wringing out his shorts at the top of the slide. "Let's try it."

I followed him up and we grasped hands. He pulled me into another kiss. Then we launched ourselves down the slide. The same grit caught at our skin, but this time I was too distracted by Eli's enthusiasm. He made goofy faces at me and I laughed. We splashed together at the bottom. The cold water tempered our shared enthusiasm, but we pawed at each other nonetheless.

I broke away and swam. Growing up in swimming pools, this playful ritual was familiar, though it's never lost its thrill. Boy teases, girl swims away. Boy endeavors to catch girl. But I was a strong swimmer and learned young that if I wanted to be caught, I had to let them catch me.

Eli caught me near the edge of the pool. I held onto the bricks, and he pressed himself against my back, kissing my neck. He ran his hands down my back and tickled between my legs. We could have fucked right there, and in retrospect I wish we had. But I was cold and nervous and decided we needed to go home.

Putting on clothes made no sense, so I walked to the fence in my bra and underwear. He launched me again but my arms were weak from the excitement. I barely caught myself at the top. I once again threw my leg over the cross bar and my underwear snagged on a small imperfection in the metal. When I pressed myself forward, my underwear stayed, yanking to the side to expose my vulva in its entirety to Eli below. I could feel him looking at this most inelegant display, but I had to focus on not breaking my neck. I swooped my other leg over and leapt to the ground, a new draft coming through the huge hole in the crotch of my panties.

We walked back to his house in our underwear, my pussy lips dangling free in the wind. It was so late we saw no one on the twenty minute walk.

Back in his apartment, he gave me a fluffy towel that I pressed against the cold damp skin of my breasts and ass, where my soaked undergarments kept me from drying naturally.

He handed me a pair of khakis and a t-shirt, both of which fit me quite well. I threw them on as he made us grilled cheese.

Cozy and comforted, we wasted no more time getting into bed. We tossed our dry clothes to the ground. A single lamp illuminated the room, warm and gentle.

"You wanna fuck?" he asked, like a Boston bro asking if I wanted a beer.

"Yeah," I mocked. "I wanna." He rolled a condom down his not-at-all-flaccid cock.

I straddled him and slid down on him. I leaned back, covering my large breasts with my arms, ashamed. I rarely liked being on top for this reason. They hung, aggressively heavy.

I would often hold them, presumably for the eroticism, but more to save me from the humiliation of their weight.

Eli grasped my hands and pulled them away. "Your tits look so fucking hot."

Crude, sure. But until that point, I'd never had a lover talk dirty nor compliment my breasts beyond shocked, silent awe.

"So hot," he repeated. "You know what you are?" he said as we fucked. "Luscious. You're fucking luscious." He punctuated the repetition with a hearty smack on my ass. This was also the first time I had been spanked.

I quickly learned that Eli was a filthy but honest boy, a combination which I so desperately required. Bless those college boys who resist objectification and misogyny. But double bless those boys who know how to do that while still being dirty bastards.

We fucked filthily and honestly for the rest of the night. It's amazing how much we could rely on our perfect young bodies to fill in the blanks of knowledge and skill.

The next morning Eli and I showered together. I enjoyed another first as he sudsed my groin and scrubbed my back. As I got dressed, he made chocolate chip pancakes. We carried them downstairs to the front porch, another lovely asset to those old Victorians in town. He had make the pancakes in the shape of Mickey Mouse, a trick he told me he learned from his father.

For the rest of breakfast we talked about summer plans and travel intentions, of exes and art and dance.

The next night I saw him at a celebration in the town square. We were both with friends. We flirted with glances from a distance, our faces illuminated by the colored Chinese lanterns that hung from the trees.

He grinned and winked as if to ask if we could do it again. I shook my head, no. I preferred to keep that adventurous night as it was, with scrapes and bruises as my mementos.

players

Setting: The Berkshires. 2002. Summer.

The players:

Alexandra: New York City actress. Aggressive in a bisexual vampire kind of way

Allison: The bisexual slutty stoner from the hippie school

Earl: The sweet but simple innkeeper

Kevin: The virgin

By the third year of my college career, I had gotten used to Friday night escapades that could have been scripted by bad porn writers.

"You have such nice boobs! Can I feel them? Here, feel mine!"

That kind of thing.

I headed off to summer stock expecting to keep this trend going. After all, summer stock is basically spring break for theater nerds. It's dozens of ensembles of hot, talented people coming together to make art in the woods for three months. How could I not get laid?

There's a lot of great performance that happens in the Berkshires in the summer: Molière, Shakespeare, light opera, ballet, symphonies, and on and on. The show I was working on was not any of those things. I interned at a dinner theater musical revue that satirized current events. It was the kind of show that used the song La Bamba to parody the India/Pakistan conflict. Real classy stuff. Each table had a different "topical" name, like "The White House," "Gaza," and "Silicon Valley."

At this show, we had two main customers: Old New York theater queens and older New York theater Jews. One night, I was working the door when one of the latter kinds of patrons refused to sit at her assigned table, Palestine.

"How can I sit at a table," she exclaimed, "that *doesn't exist?!*"

The production housed all the interns in a ski lodge in a tiny town called Otis. The residents of Otis had bumper stickers on their cars that said "Notice Otis." It wasn't a touristy thing. It was a desperate plea for recognition.

Our lodging, as everything related to the interns, was clearly a way to stretch a budget to its breaking point while squeezing out as much underpaid labor as possible. The ski lodge was likely beautiful with a light dusting of snow, but at the height of summer it looked like a shrunken version of the hotel in *The Shining*. The place was called The Grouse House, but we interns took to calling it the Gross Houss.

The rooms were upstairs, and the downstairs held a bar and restaurant. I never saw anyone in the bar or restaurant other than Earl. When he didn't have anything better to do, Earl would bartend for us, which just added to the whole

Shining ambiance.

Earl was a tall, grizzled man. He was, as country folk would say, "simple." I don't mean that as an insult; he was just a simple dude who tended to the Gross Houss in a white undershirt and sweatpants. I envied him. Earl was both sweet and creepy in that horror movie way, where you didn't know if he was the serial killer or the dude who'd save everyone at the end with a well-timed shovel to the killer's head. He liked the company of us four college rapscallions, particularly since three of the four of us were pretty girls. Earl was simple, but he was no fool.

On the first night in the Gross Houss, we lost an intern after Earl told us about George, the Native American ghost who lived upstairs. Lucille was back in her car so fast, she didn't even turn her head when she said, "Black folk don't suffer ghosts."

Lucille was replaced by Alexandra, a New York City actress who imagined herself a star. She reminded me of Carrie Bradshaw, all wacky outfits and self-importance, but brunette and stretched to nearly six feet tall.

Alexandra and I got along because we both loved drugs and sex. These two things have a way of bridging even the widest gap between women. The problem was, all the good drugs were still in New York, and the only thing with a reasonable cock in a twenty mile radius was Kevin, the virgin. Neither Alexandra nor Kevin were my type, but summer stock has a way of changing a woman.

Kevin was a classic musical theater virgin: the kind of guy whose own mother assumed was gay, whose first kiss was a stage kiss, and whose idea of a good time was transcribing Top 40 hits for his a cappella group. Being a posh kid, Kevin brought a big TV and video games to the Gross Houss. When it was his shift at the theater, he let me play Legend of Zelda in his room.

I had slept with virgins before, but I'd since sworn them off. They were never, ever worth the trouble.

Alexandra seemed resolved, however, to make that cock carry her through the humid Massachusetts summer.

One afternoon I was swashbuckling through Hyrule with a joint hanging from my lips when Kevin rushed into the room, sweaty and awkward. I didn't think anyone else was home but took his weirdness as my cue to save and quit.

I went to the kitchenette to find Alexandra, fighting with a bag of baby carrots. This kind of low-level drama continued for a few days until I realized something was going on.

Everything came to head on the fourth of July. It was a brutally humid night, and the interns celebrated our nation's birth by drinking Yellow Tail out of the bottle in our underwear, holding sparklers.

We went on a drunken twilight walk through the eerily quiet town, climbed a tree in the Otis cemetery, and talked trash about the actors and producers of the show.

Back at the Gross Houss, the fourth intern passed out, leaving me, Alexandra, and Kevin in his room. The three of us undressed and started making out. To my delight, Alexandra was a good kisser and had a phenomenal body, too often hidden by tutus and pleather corsets.

At this point I think it's important to acknowledge that queer women hate being exoticized by straight guys. The whole, "Let's make out to get these guys horny" is an obnoxious trend that puts our sexuality fully in the realm of patriarchal sex fantasy, and most of us resent it. That said, when the straight dude is a virgin, it can be pretty funny to watch his brain explode. Alexandra seemed to be on the same page with me on that.

I cuddled up on one side of Kevin while Alexandra was on the other. She and leaned over to kiss above his chest. I reached over his bare torso and slid my fingers into Alexandra, giving Kevin a friendly tug along the way. Kevin stared in wide-eyed wonder at Alexandra's face as it moved through contortions of pleasure he had obviously yet to see. She moaned and squealed as she came on my hand.

Alexandra cooed, coming down from her orgasm. She returned to lucidity just in time to hear Kevin grunt and moan.

I glanced down to see his belly covered in jizz. Alexandra and I shared a confused look. We had barely touched the kid.

Really? we said to each other with a silent look.

Figuring he was going to have to sit this game out for the next five to ten minutes, I crawled over his chest so I could lay on top of Alexandra and get better leverage. We kept fucking until Kevin was hard again. Though I hadn't been particularly attracted to Alexandra, and I'm sure she felt the same way about me, sex with her felt like a fun diversion, a minor escape from the celibate hellscape that was summerstock in the Birkshires. We enjoyed a slutty solidarity, and it was our duty to support each other through those dark days and dry nights.

At this point I figured I should tap out and let Alexandra take the lead, so I excused myself with some pecks on the lips and went back to my room.

The shouts from Kevin's room continued. I slipped my Velvet Goldmine DVD in my laptop for a little soft-core dandy-on-dandy action, rolled a joint, and cranked open the windows. Warm night air and Al Green on the bar's stereo wafted into my room. I jacked off. Nothing quite like Christian Bale taking it up the ass from Ewan McGregor to get the juices flowing, amirite? I enjoyed a loud, boisterous orgasm, containing a whole summer's worth of sexual frustration, to let the kids down the hall know I was still appreciating their vibe. Alexandra responded with another gregarious orgasm.

I picked up my laptop, pulled down the sheets to get into bed, and discovered a giant earwig on my pillow. I screamed.

"You okay, Allison?" a man's voice queried.

"Yeah," I called out, trying to calm my blood chemistry. "Just a bug."

My panic passed and I looked around, wondering where the voice came from. It wasn't Kevin.

I stuck my head out my open window. On the deck just below, Earl was entertaining the first guests the Gross Houss had seen all summer. Dinner and cocktails all around. Earl looked up and smiled.

"You having a fun fourth?" he asked, a cheeky grin on his stubbled face.

The seven patrons at the table looked up too.

I waved, hoping the night hid my blush. "Um. Okay. Happy Fourth."

Kevin and Alexandra's romance didn't last the summer. Alexandra and I never hooked up again either. Like many queers before me, I ended up having to visit NYC to get properly laid.

But Kevin did finally bid adieu to the big V, which warms my heart.

At the curtain of that summer, all I can add is,

If my words have offended,
think of this and all is mended.
A musical theater virgin is no more,
once he has the chance
to enjoy a good score.

heroes and villains

THE LORD OF the Rings changed my life.

My freshman year of college I walked into my boyfriend David's dorm room while he was on the phone with a friend from LA. The friend had recently arrived in New Zealand for this series of film shoots. He was telling David about all the crazy concept drawings and costumes and getting the star treatment and meeting all these big name actors. I had no idea what they were talking about, but it sounded pretty damn cool.

After the call, David said that was his friend Elijah from Los Angeles, and he's playing a big role in this series of movies based on this series of books. The Lord of the Rings, he thinks it's called?

Two years later, I sat in a movie theater with a bunch of my college friends. We'd smuggled in a bunch of beer and were settling in to watch *The Fellowship of the Ring*. The whole excursion was led by my friend Nick, a total Tolkien-head, who knew the canon inside and out. Meanwhile, I knew nothing about the books or story. I hadn't read them growing up, so I went into the film with a complete beginner's mind, except for the essential tidbits Nick has given me on the car ride over.

The lights lowered, and from the first sound cue, I was hooked. I was swept into this world and it was so compelling. Gandalf fell into the mines and I screamed, "No!!!" I cried and kept crying for the rest of the movie. On the ride home Nick bitched about everything the film did wrong, but my mind was still traveling the paths of Middle Earth.

A year later I was back in the same movie theater with the same friends and same amount of beer. Gandalf was back and we cheered! He showed up on his horse and it was the first light of the fifth day and Gandalf saved the day and we all sobbed with pride and relief. My friends and I held hands while Sam talked about the great stories, the ones that really matter, tears streaming down our faces.

I had never been so moved by a film before. It felt like Stendhal Syndrome. I was out of my ego, my consciousness floating somewhere between my body and the world that I was watching on the screen. I fell so hard for *The Lord of the Rings*.

A few months after seeing *The Two Towers*, I was invited to a costume party with the theme "Heroes and Villains." As I prepared for the party, I decided to channel my inner androgynous boy. I found myself layers of leather and wool in browns and greens, conditioned my long blond hair, and tossed on a cape. I became Legolas.

Legolas represented everything I wanted to be. He was brave, beautiful, intuitive, skilled at fighting, and in tune with nature. He was the dream man. I wanted to be him, I wanted to fuck him, I wanted it all.

It was a great party. I watched a male Hermione make out with a female Snape on the couch. Dr. No danced with Captain Underpants. Pussy Galore and Storm did acroyoga in the corner. I flirted with three different Harry Potters of varying genders. I felt sexy and strong and got endless compliments on my costume.

The party was across campus from my house, so the walk home was a long one. On the way, I cut through the main town square. It was one of those normal small town squares: a bucolic green space with trees, a gazebo and various paths. It was three a.m. and the whole place was deserted.

Before I go further, I should note that I had never heard of "LARPing" before. I had never heard of cosplay. I had a vague notion that some of my pagan friends played an intricate game involving twenty-sided dice, but that was the extent of this kind of nerd knowledge.

I had also been a bit of a serious kid, so even when I played, I had my ego watching me and sort of making fun of me in the background. As far back as I can remember, I had never had an experience of playful immersion.

So imagine my surprise, as I walked through this empty park at three a.m., to find myself stalked by a twenty foot tall troll.

I didn't really know what to do with that.

I didn't know what to do, other than run. And hide. And duck. And dodge. And pull an arrow from my quiver and fire. And miss. And try again, and hit!

On this long walk home, I leapt over boulders and hid behind trees and nocked arrows and fought enemies. I was in full LARP mode.

Thirty minutes later, I reached home—my Rivendell—which was a crappy rental house on the north end of campus, but I didn't feel *done.* My journey had not been satisfied. I had not vanquished enough foes.

I stood at my front door at three-thirty a.m. in full costume, and instead of going to bed like a reasonable human, I pocketed my keys and walked back to Middle Earth, like a warrior elf.

I ran back to the town square feeling like I was the only person on the planet, let alone this tiny Ohio town. I played so long that I exhausted myself.

Then I found my tree. This was a special tree for me. I had spent a lot of time studying under this tree. I processed my big break up there. I cuddled with other sweeties there. Now it was my senior year, and it occurred to me that I had yet to *climb* this tree.

I climbed the tree. About fifteen feet up, I found a nice thick branch and straddled it like a leopard. I wrapped my cape around me and relaxed into the branch. It felt cozy and safe up there.

I let my body ease into the branch and rest. I watched the rising moon and cherished the silence.

Then the tree made a pass at me.

I'm wasn't sure how to feel. But I was into it. So I made a pass right back. My body started getting warm, and the tree got warm. I wriggled against the branch, and the branch wriggled right back. It was on.

I humped the branch between my legs until I came. The energy from my orgasm shot out of my body, down the branch, down the trunk, and into the earth. Then the earth returned it with amazing fervor, up the trunk and up the branch and into my body. I got dizzy and high. I fucked a tree.

Then I promptly fell asleep.

I woke up to the gibbous moon bright above me. Despite the depth of the night, I felt vulnerable and exposed. Instead of dropping down and doing the four-thirty a.m. walk of shame like any normal person, I climbed higher. Like a warrior elf.

I found a forked branch and I lay back on it. It perfectly cradled my shoulders and felt like a strong arm holding me along my spine. I wrapped my legs around the trunk, and I felt the tree's excitement again.

"You are insatiable," I said to the tree. I rubbed myself against it again and fell back asleep.

I woke hours later to full morning. The park was filled with people. I heard a rustling below and rolled over to find my theater professor walking his dog, Yeti. Yeti was pissing on my lover. I would have been offended, but I suspected the tree was cool with it.

I looked out at all the people and realized that despite the crowd, I was still alone. No one saw me. No one looked up.

So I jacked off again.

I put my hand down my Legolas-leggings and pulled it out, soaked with my arousal. I wiped my juicy hand on the branch, giving some of me back to the tree.

Seconds later, an ant crawled up to my little puddle of cum and drank. He walked away, followed by another ant that drank from the puddle, and then another and another. A whole little army of ants was drinking my cum. Before I could get too creeped out, I remembered that I was wearing an elf outfit and had slept in a tree. This seemed pretty par for the course. I rolled with it.

I realized that I should probably go home and take a shower and eat something or else I might just float away. I wondered if I should wait for the park to clear out a bit, but I doubted that would happen anytime soon. So I climbed down and dropped from the lowest branch.

No one batted an eye as a blond girl in a Legolas costume dropped from a tree. Then I remembered why I enrolled in a hippie school.

A few months later was Drag Ball, the biggest party on campus. I dusted off my cape and boots and convinced my ex-girlfriend and two friends to compete in the drag show with me as the Fellowship of the Schwing. My ex dressed as Aragorn, and on stage in front of the whole school—students and professors alike—I dropped to my knees and fellated Aragorn's sword. Gollum ripped off Frodo's shirt, looking for the ring. Geeky bedlam ensued. We ended up placing 2nd in the competition.

That night I got properly laid, as one should expect after a party where all the boys wear short, tight dresses, and all the girls wear mustaches and neckties. The sex was mediocre, but I sleep well in my partner's arms nonetheless.

The next morning I woke unsatisfied. I kicked my partner to the curb.

My boots and cape stayed at home, but I had a date with my tree.

polyglot

My lover Joey and I decided we wanted to start fucking other people. To be fair we already were fucking other people, but we wanted to do it around the same time in around the same place. So when he moved from Los Angeles to Barcelona, I did what any best-friend-with-benefits would do and bought a ticket to join him there.

Immediately we were having a ball. We fashioned ourselves bohemian writer types recapturing a romantic prewar era of European leisure and creativity. We stayed in his uncle Pepe's flat. It was a two-bedroom apartment on the top floor of a three story building, a block away from the beach. Because Barcelona is apparently the kind of place where you can own a two bedroom apartment on the top floor of a three story building a block away from the beach, on the salary of a puppeteer. If that doesn't make you want to re-examine your life choices, I don't know what will.

We spent every day on the beach. I loved letting my breasts hang free in the wind. I'm fairly sure the locals didn't mind either. One day while sunbathing I watched an old leathery woman play cards with a six year old. The woman's breasts dangled down into her lap, and when she smiled, which was often, I could see the many places where she was missing teeth. Nevertheless, the woman was radiant (and not just because her skin had absorbed so much UV). She looked like she possessed the kind of contentment one gets from spending seventy years playing cards on the beach, topless.

I wanted to be surrounded by people like that. It was a world so removed from my life in LA, where the only topless women were the surgically-enhanced, Hollywood-sanctioned types, and the only leisure is owned by those who try fencing public beaches to exclude the proletariat.

Joey and I were contemplating that woman's pendulous breasts and jagged smile when I heard a girl's voice say, "No, no, no. Not 'fah vahn.' Eet's 'vah, fahn.'"

Recognizing this as a lesson in one of my favorite Italian cusses, I shouted "Vaffanculo!"

The girl whipped her head around and laughed. Her friends laughed too. And then the three girls stood up and dragged their beach chairs to us.

Joey looked and me and whispered, "You are awesome."

"I know," I replied.

"Vaffanculo" means, essentially, "fuck off" in Italian. Literally translated, it's "go fuck the ass."

Two of the girls were Italian: a brunette named Valeria and a blonde named Sara. The third was an American named Tracy. She pronounced it with the timbre and trill of a piccolo.

The Italians took a shine to me, hopefully for more than my excellent Italian cussing skills. Tracy, meanwhile, set her sights on Joey.

When Joey got up to take a swim, Tracy started asking some innocent questions designed to drill down for details. I decided to save her the effort.

"He's not my boyfriend. And he's decent in bed," I said.

Her jaw dropped. "You are awesome," she said.

"Yeah…I know," I replied.

The five of us decided to meet up later that night to go clubbing.

The club was one of those Eurotrash places with three floors of terrible techno music, no good beer, and a twenty euro cover charge. But the hot Italians invited us, so what were we gonna do?

Tracy found me and Joey at the bar. We ordered a round of tequila shots. Before I even finished sucking the juice out of my lime, Tracy dragged Joey to the couches near the dance floor, threw him down, on started grinding on him.

That solved Joey's problem, I thought. Now Mama's gotta get laid.

I ordered another tequila shot and took a lap around the club. Downstairs I found the Italians, but they were busy mooning over some Brazilians who wouldn't give them the time of day, so I went back up to the bar. Tracy's tongue was down Joey's throat and her hand was in his pants. I ordered another tequila shot and weighed my options.

As I threw back the shot, the dance floor cleared a bit, and I saw him: an Orlando Bloom look-a-like standing on the dance floor flanked by four male friends.

Well shit, I thought. *I know what I'm doing tonight.*

I left my empty shot glass on the bar and made a beeline

for him. His friends wisely backed away. And Mr. Bloom and I started dancing. The chemistry was immediate. We even started making out a bit before we exchanged one word. Finally he pulled away and said in a thick accent, "My name ees Mateo."

Now, I don't know if it was Barcelona or the tequila or my newly discovered non-monogamous lifestyle, but I decided to make up a persona.

"Hola, Mateo, me llamo Anna," I said, emphasizing the fake name with a Catalan flair.

"Where you are from?" he asks, his "r's" rolling with a feline purr.

"Aquí," I lied. I was from here

Luckily Mateo was not from aquí or else he would have known there was no way in hell I was Catalan. But Mateo was from *Milano* and spoke zero words of Spanish and not much more of English. My secret identity was secure. And it was on.

We kept dancing and making out, and things got hotter and heavier. I decided we needed to take it onto the beach. Outside, I threw Mateo to the sand, undid his fly, hiked up my skirt, and started riding the boy.

Recalling this bit of the story inspires a question. I've never gotten a solid answer to this question, so perhaps it will be a type of Zen koan for you to contemplate later as you admire a sunset.

The question is: "What is the requisite distance that voyeurs should stand away while watching two strangers fuck on a beach?"

The one answer I know to be incorrect is: "Close enough

to smoke the cigarettes that fell out of my pocket when I hiked up my skirt."

But that's the answer I got.

It wasn't exactly a turn on.

Mateo and I reassembled our clothes and dignities and headed back to the club.

On our way in, we ran into Joey and Tracy heading out. We all cheered drunkenly at our good timing and decided to head back to the flat.

Upstairs, Joey showed Tracy into our room, I showed Mateo into the guest room, and Joey and I convened in the kitchen to get everyone some water.

Watching Joey pour four glasses of water for us, I was hit with a strong sense of gratitude. I was finally engaging in the ethical non-monogamous relationship that I'd always wanted. I was so grateful to have this awesome lover who wasn't jealous or angry or judgey. He was happy to be on this adventure with me, and I with him.

Almost to confirm my feelings and make sure I wasn't making all of this up, I said, "Joey, you know I love you, right?"

"Of course," he replied. "I love you, too."

We kissed.

Then we started making out.

We made out in the kitchen for about five minutes before we remembered we had other people waiting for us in our bedrooms.

Back in the bedroom, Mateo and I picked up right where we left off on the beach, sans creepsters.

I tried to communicate what I wanted in the smattering

of restaurant Italian that I knew. The word "ecco" came in handy. It means "here."

I was also delighted to use my favorite Italian cuss word for the second time that day, this time in its more literal, and pleasurable, form.

Right around the time Mateo was obliging my *culo* request, I started to come. At this point I'd completely forgotten that I was supposed to be Anna from Barcelona instead of Allie from Cleveland. If Mateo had noticed, he was smart enough to keep his mouth shut.

As I started to come, however, I remembered my secret identity. So, in my increasing fervor, I decided to recommit to the character.

Instead of coming "normal style," you know, the whole, "Oh god, oh god, yes, yes, YES!!!," I went for something a little bit different.

"Ay! ay! ay! O, dios! Aquí! Aquí! Sí, sí, SÍÍÍÍÍÍÍ!"

I'm not proud.

But it was hilarious.

After, Mateo and I cuddled and shared pillow talk in the style of developmentally disabled six year olds.

"You know," he said, "I can go to Dublin."

"Um, what?"

"I can usual go to Dublin."

I stared at him, wondering if I was about to get ditched in a most international style.

"You know," he said. "More than one."

"Oh!" I shouted. "Double! Twice! You can go twice."

"Twice." He rolled the word around on his beautiful tongue.

"Twice," I repeated. "Okay. Let's go!"

Mateo and I were done going to Dublin around dawn. Afterward, we headed into the living room for a cigarette. Tracy and Joey joined moments later. The four of us shared a sleepy half-conversation. Joey showed Mateo how to get back to his hostel. I talked to Tracy about, I dunno, her shoes or something.

I walked Mateo to the door. We kissed and said our half-cogent goodbyes. As he walked away, Mateo turned over his shoulder and said "Hola," before walking into the Barcelona sunrise.

While Joey showed Tracy out, I stripped off my clothes and scurried into Joey's and my bed.

Joey returned and nestled in to spoon to me.

"How was it?" I asked.

"Eh," he said. "She said she liked me too much to fuck me, so she gave me a blow job."

"Poor baby," I said, scooting my ass close to his cock.

"How about you?" he asked.

"Well," I said. "I got fucked in the ass for the first time and it made me come like a girl from a Reggeton song."

He laughed. "You're awesome."

"I know."

Joey scooted closer to me and I felt him get hard. We fucked. It was the hottest, most honest fuck we'd ever shared.

Afterward, I rested my head on his chest and said, "Hey Joey, would you like to go to Dublin?"

sunset stripped

Los Angeles has many things going for it. Sunshine. Ceviche. Ab density per square mile. However, brains, feminism, and gender-non-conformity are not among those things.

Three months after graduating with a neuroscience degree I was already certain I'd never use, I moved to Los Angeles for the vague promise of a job in television. The job was as a production assistant on a one-hour family drama on the WB, back when the WB was a network that hosted high-art like "America's Next Top Model" and "The Jamie Kennedy Experiment." A production assistant is essentially a peon, a grunt, a mote. A worthless piece of human trash whose existence is only to serve teenage prima donnas and their stage mothers. And make photocopies.

Los Angeles proved a difficult landing place after a near-idyllic Midwestern upbringing. It was a city that attempted to give me an eating disorder under the guise of building me into a stronger person.

To be fair, it wasn't just that I was working and living

in Los Angeles, it was that I was working in Hollywood and living on the Sunset Strip. When I first moved into my apartment, my roommate Jill took me to her bedroom window and pointed down at the sidewalk. She said, "That's where River died."

Living across the street from the Viper Room may sound "LA glamorous" except when it takes five hours to get home because the Lakers won or you want to buy some damn tampons and Hägen Dazs but can't get to the register because eight groupies are fighting over who gets to buy Anthony Kiedis's cigarettes.

My roommate, Jill, was a total party girl. She loved hitting the clubs up and down the strip every weekend. She dated and/or slept with most of the bartenders, which for me meant free drinks. I hated partying on the Strip, but it was my neighborhood, and I was a broke ass P.A. who liked getting drunk for free.

The hardest part about those first seven months in LA was that I was working a super stressful job that kept me running around fourteen hours a day, and I wasn't getting laid. I had gone from bountiful queer, pansexual utopia in the middle of Ohio, to dry as a desert in Los Angeles. In LA, the women wouldn't sleep with me because I was bisexual and therefore a "cocksucker." The men wouldn't sleep with me because—well, they *would* sleep with me, but I thought they were disgusting.

I couldn't go out for a drink without getting unsolicited advice like "Wear tighter jeans" or "If you want to make it in the industry, you should lose fifteen pounds." The weirdest part was I wasn't trying to "make it in the industry." These guys just saw blond hair and big boobs and naturally assumed that was my goal.

Thus, I didn't get laid for a long time.

After a while, though, I needed to remedy the situation. The lack of sex was getting to be problematic. I was wound so tight I worried another batch of script rewrites or unsolicited beauty advice might make me snap. So I did what most normal people do when they need to get laid: I lowered my standards.

One Friday night, Jill invites me out. Rather than my usual jeans and a t-shirt, I put on the tightest shirt, shortest skirt, and highest heels I own. We go to a club called Bliss. Rumor is Hugh Hefner is going to be there, and he is, along with his blondtourage. Everyone is trying to get Hugh's attention, while I'm just trying to get the bartender's attention.

I have a few drinks to kill the pain in the balls of my feet from those stupid high heels. Then I wait in an interminable line for the bathroom. To this day, I believe that all LA clubs should have two lines for the bathrooms: one for needing to actually pee, and the other for cocaine. It would cut down on everyone's impatience with the others' urgent needs.

There is an equally long line for the men's room (because of cocaine). Across from me is a light-skinned black man with green eyes, full mauve lips, and long, perfect dreadlocks. His legs are likewise crossed.

We start talking, and he's kind and funny and smart, and I think, *I've got to lock this down.*

Jill finds me and wants to bounce to a new bar that's catty-corner from our apartment. Perfect. The place is called Red Rock and it's a "dive bar" in that all the bartenders wear plaid. I'm from Ohio. A dive bar there is where there are peanut shells on the ground and they don't serve anything in glass in case a fight breaks out. That's a dive bar, this was an overpriced model hangout with crappy beer. But I guess I'm splitting hairs.

I invite Mr. Beautiful, whose name is John, and he agrees to come with. We enter the bar and start dancing. It's obviously on. We move together beautifully and have killer chemistry. Eventually the pain in my feet grows unbearable and I decide I want to be on my back. I invite him home with me. He agrees, but first he wants to stop at his hotel. We head down the street to the Mondrian where he and his coworkers are staying. John says he's a cameraman on a reality show in town for the night. I don't know if that's true, and I don't care. Either way, he had an expense account, so along with his "film crew," we raid the mini-fridge.

Then someone whips out some cocaine and I try it for the first time. I actually half try it because I don't know you have to hold your breath as you get close, or else you end up snuffing all of the powder off the table. Happily for me (less so for my new friends) I get just enough cocaine in my system to get horny and ego-emboldened. I decide we need to go home and fuck right. Now.

John and I walk back down the street to my apartment, head to my room, and start tearing at each other. It's the kind of drunken, cocaine-y sex that's ravenous and brazen and wild. John is even more beautiful naked. He has an amazing body and a beautiful cock. When he lies back on my pillow, his dreadlocks splay around his head. He looks like a sexy lion, and all I want to do is make him growl.

We have the kind of sex where I don't know if want to keep my eyes closed because it feels so good or keep my eyes open because it looks so good.

I had an amazing panorama view from my bedroom window of Hollywood, West Hollywood, and Beverly Hills. I'd lie in bed at night just wanting to look at that view while getting fucked from behind and finally, FINALLY it was happening.

The sex goes all night…I think.

The next morning I wake up with my head on my pillow. John is lying opposite me with his head at the foot of the bed. Our legs are intertwined, and our genitals are still lined up. Apparently we'd passed out, simultaneously, while having sex. There's something I can check off my Bucket list.

I drop John off at his hotel so we can both properly tend our hangovers with Saturday brunch, the way Los Angeles intended.

Monday night, I go out to celebrate a friend's birthday. We tear it up, as was often the case with that group of guys. I end up on the birthday boy's couch, since I'm too drunk to drive. As I drift off to sleep, a part of my brain I usually don't allow to function late at night sounds a tiny alarm. That alarm reminds me that I have the earliest call time of the season the next morning. I have to be at the office at five a.m. I look at my cell phone. It is currently 3:15. I get sick. I throw up. And I fall asleep.

Forty-five minutes later, my actual alarm goes off. I stumble to my feet, chug a glass of water, and drive to the office.

I am greeted at the office by a stack of rewrites waiting on my desk, which I have to copy and collate before the cast and crew show up.

The relationship a P.A. has with their photocopier is like what the Navi in *Avatar* have with those dragon things. "I see you," I whisper to the copier. It chirps in response, then chokes on a stack of blue paper and jams in four places to prove its devotion to me.

I remove flakes of toner-caked blue paper while wearing the same outfit I wore the night before: hoodie, heels, and denim miniskirt. The lead teamster, a thick-calved redhead, is the only other crew member on set. He walks past the copy room and eyes me. "If you gotta be hungover," he says, "you may as well get paid for it.

"I'll let you know when the hangover *starts*," I snarl.

Fifteen hours later, I'm still on set. Our episode director thinks of himself as an auteur, setting up each shot of this terrible family dramedy as though it were a Kubrickian masterpiece to be studied in film classes for generations. We've had three rounds of rewrites for no reason. I usually empathize with the struggle for editorial perfection, but I promise, the script of this show *did not matter.*

All the other P.A.'s had come and gone. I'm working a double shift, and all I want is to hear the walkie-talkie screech with the words, "Martini shot." But instead I hear the dreaded words, "Rewrites." I unload a ream of buttercup paper, a sign of how many rewrites we've already had. Somewhere after six other colors and between buttercup and double white is when you know Los Angeles has you by the short hairs. I eye the box of white paper, whispering an incantation that repeats the word "Martini shot." My Los Angeles life feels more bleak by the moment. I load up the copier with buttercup paper. My trembling fingers struggle to reach for a handful of brads.

I recall a Raymond Pettibon painting that I once saw in a museum with the inscription, "I thought California would be different." But I didn't think that. Even though the details were sketchy, I somehow knew it would be just like this: hungover in last night's miniskirt, flecks of dried vomit in my hoodie, catering to the overinflated egos of people getting paid ten times what I did to recite pointless lines while holding prop surfboards.

I run between the copy room and my office. It's a long corridor with a lobby in between the two. By now I've taken off my shoes (which the assistant director reminds me is against OSHA rules) and I'm half running, half stomping down the hall.

I run to the copier to clear the paper jam and grab the fresh scripts, then stomp them back to my office to collate and brad them together. Then back to the copy room and back to the office.

Halfway from my office on the final trip, I feel something go wrong in my body. My pelvis feels weird, off, *bad.* I stop in the lobby and hold my abdomen waiting for it to pass, but it doesn't. Out of instinct, I reach into my skirt, into my underwear, and up into my vagina.

I feel something. I reach deeper and grab it with my fingers. And pull. I'm pulling slowly and it feels like my vagina is turning itself inside out. *Oh god, oh god.* I pull this *whatever* out of my vagina. I pull and pull, and finally, dangling between my fingers, is a condom.

I am disgusted and horrified and slightly amused, but

mostly horrified. I stand, stunned, staring at this shriveled bit of orange latex. Then I realize, I am standing in the lobby of my office building holding a four-day old condom I just fished out of my cunt.

I run to the bathroom with a rush of adrenaline and rage and whip that sucker into the toilet. I stand over the toilet and see everything that's wrong with my life in LA—my job, my body image, my sexual identity, my social life—is wrapped up inside that pathetic piece of latex. I decide to make some changes. First, drink less. Second, look for a new job. And third, and most importantly, I'm going to try being a lesbian for a little while.

good dyke

BEFORE I IDENTIFIED as a queer, I identified as a lesbian. Before I identified as a lesbian, I identified as a greedy bisexual. It was easy to identify as a greedy bisexual in college, because I went to a hippie liberal arts school where the women were brainy, feminist, artistic, and gender non-conforming, and the men were brainy, feminist, artistic, and gender-non-conforming too. It made it really easy to want to fuck them all. So I did. Or at least I tried.

When I moved to Los Angeles, I had no reason to think any of these things would change. Sure, I had visited LA, but the shallowness of the "industry" never sunk in. The difference between my rural hippie liberal arts school and the film-fueled megalopolis wouldn't become clear to me for a few months. During those months, broke and miserable, I wrote off my malaise as normal growing pains. But then I started paying more attention to the people around me, how they talked to me and one another.

On the set of the TV show where I worked, my

appearance was always an available conversation topic. Women, whether talent or crew, were constantly weighed and measured against some unspoken standard. They'd run casting calls for background girls in bikinis just for fun.

It wasn't much easier outside of work. One of my two good friends hit on me whenever we drank. It had become so routine that shooting him down felt more and more like waving a joint past without taking a hit. The other friend read my diary and waited for a particularly vulnerable time to mock me. My female friends would grip the back of my jeans to show me how they were too baggy and say they didn't want to go out with me if I wouldn't put more attention into the way I dressed.

Rather than suffer the indignities of these "friendships," I often took long nighttime walks to entertain myself. The solitude of walking in LA was a marvel. Cars whizzed by, frustration seeping through their windows like thrummy bass, and I was all alone on the pristine sidewalks.

One such night I wandered into a store called Grand Opening, a new sex toy store geared to women. Living in West Hollywood, I was familiar with sex toy stores, but they were all black lacquer and smoked mirrors. This was well lit and staffed by lesbians. I was confused but thrilled.

I didn't know what to look for, nor did I have much money to spend. But I knew I wanted something, anything, to signal that this was a place for me. I walked slowly past the vibrators, admiring their cute colors and shapes. Caterpillars! Dolphins! Then I browsed the dildos and harnesses. I had yet to use a strap-on and, without a girlfriend, held no real curiosity for them either. Against the back wall, near the black leather bondage gear, I saw a display of flaccid penises in a range of colors and sizes. The dyke at the counter walked over and explained these were soft packers.

"They have no real sexual use. They're used for gender play, when you want to have that bulge, y'know?"

I picked one up and felt it wiggle in my hand. It was soft, squishy, and realistic looking—the polar opposite of the candy colored vibrators on the wall behind me. I grabbed the light, medium sized one and took it to the register.

The clerk persuaded me that it wasn't a sex toy and didn't really do anything. I handed her my cash anyway. I was embarrassed by my lack of knowledge, but curious about this strange object above all the others that thrummed and buzzed.

At home I placed the packer in my Hanes briefs. I had always enjoyed wearing the undergarments assigned to the other gender, another source of mockery from my female friends. I could easily explain my underwear preference as one of comfort, but whether it was physical or emotional comfort, I didn't know.

With the bulge in my underwear, I felt extraordinary. I grasped and adjusted it like I imagined I would do if it were real. I put on my baggiest jeans (given to me by a painter lover in college), changed into a sports bra, and shuffled under the sink for an ACE bandage.

I bound my breasts—no small feat for my double D's—and turned to the side to admire my smoother profile. I brushed my long blond hair off my shoulder to improve the view. Then I grimaced. I was nearing a certain kind of rightness, but there was something left to alter. I rummaged through my desk for my orange-handled scissors. I returned to the bathroom, tied my hair into a braid as I had seen done on those makeover TV shows. Then I pressed the scissors against the nape of my neck and cut the braid free. It fell to the sink. I shook out my new short haircut and smirked.

I put on a baggy flannel shirt and laced my black combat boots tight. Then I headed back out. The sidewalks were just as empty as before, but this time I strode proudly. I loved the heft I felt in my underwear and the lightness on my neck and chest.

In retrospect, I'm sure I looked to passersby just like any other dyke, but I felt boyish. Masculine, even.

I walked proud and unafraid late into the night.

Blisters tugged at my feet as I climbed the steps back to my apartment. I threw myself on my bed and reached into my underwear, unbuttoning my fly to let my cock flop out.

I licked my hand and stroked my cock. Of course it didn't get hard. But it didn't need to. I played with it and jerked it off as though it were mine and not just a sex toy. With my left hand I pressed the balls hard against my mound while I stroked with my right. I slowed down and sped up like I imagined I would had my cock been flesh.

Soon after that, I quit my shitty TV job. A series of equally shitty jobs followed, but I took strides to improve my social life.

My first excellent choice was to stop dating men. Moreover, I decided to stop caring about what men thought, fullstop. I hadn't spent much mind on them to begin with (hence the baggy jeans and such), but making a conscious choice to root out and eradicate any outposts men had in my head was incredibly liberating. Free from the yoke of trying to impress imbeciles, I started going to clubs where my fashion choices were considered hot, not outré. I wasn't expected to skip meals or drink only clear alcohol. I could wear makeup and be "edgy" or no makeup and be normal.

I could dance all night because I wore comfortable shoes.

I used a now defunct social media site to find other queer women, and I was delighted to find out one of my old middle school friends was a Los Angeles-residing muff diver. We started going out together. Her extroverted nature was the perfect accompaniment to my timid social style. More than once, I would sic her on girls I thought were cute, and she'd return like Lassie, a phone number in her hand.

Slowly my confidence built. I discovered, covered in sweat, tit to tit with girls who would become either fond memories or lifelong friends, that being a dyke wasn't just eating pussy. It was a culture, a sisterhood, a mutual understanding. Dyke community had its own standards for beauty, friendship, and sex. Its rules made sense to me, and I embraced them fully. Dyke community showed me that I wasn't the wrong kind of woman. I had been hanging with the wrong kind of people. I wasn't a greedy bisexual or a hopeless case. I was a dyke.

sacred union

My sister had the good sense and decency to plan her bridal shower to coincide with my five-year college reunion. It required me to buy only one plane ticket from Los Angeles to Cleveland, and it promised plenty of mimosas to kill the hangover I was sure to have at the brunch-time affair.

Being a broke-ass bastard, I decided to forgo renting a dorm room for the weekend, choosing instead to rent an SUV and camp in the back. Issues of showering, shitting, and sexing would be dealt with in the same way I dealt with them in college—by mooching off my friends.

I packed a sleeping bag, one decent dress and heels, and a bunch of my usual crummy jeans and tees.

I drove to Oberlin and parked in the lot I used to get ticketed in when I was a student, flipping off the sign that said "faculty parking only" for nostalgia's sake. I bought no tickets and had no badge. I was just there for the booze and two nights of regrettable choices.

Soon after I arrived, I found an old friend heading in my

direction. Ashley was a smart-ass from D.C. We went skinny dipping together the night after we met at freshman orientation, with a bunch of other dorm-mates. She made snarky comments about the water quality of Lake Erie, but I could tell it was out of love.

The first time I got arrested, she was there shouting at the asshole cop. She was also always willing to tell a dude what was what in either English or Spanish, ratchet or high-society—whichever got the point across best.

At reunions, folks are partial to nostalgia, and Ashley and I wasted no time before gossiping and snarking over drinks. She was the queen of shade, chatty with anyone until she turned away to reveal her real feelings with a curled lip or rolled eyes. I loved her.

On one of our cross-campus walks, looking for trouble, I bemoaned the fact that I never had sex in the library. It was a rite of passage to fuck in the library, specifically in a special kind of chair called a "womb chair," which was a mod-ish retro chair that was so-named because it forced you to curl your knees up to your chin just to sit down. Some claimed they were so comforting and cozy, they were perfect for naps. I just thought they smelled like mildew and white-people dreadlocks.

"Dang!" Ashley shouted. "I never did that either! I feel like I missed out."

Though the library was clearly closed—it was 1.a.m. and the lights were off—Ashley grasped my wrist and dragged me up the ramp to the front doors. She yanked at the doors, which clinked against their chains.

"Fuckers. Shouldn't kids be studying for their finals?"

"Commencement is in two days," I said.

"Whatever. Lazy asses."

She dragged me back down the ramp and to the basement entrance. The doors were likewise sealed.

She harrumphed.

"Were you really going to fuck me if we could get inside?" I asked.

"Hell yeah! That'd be a story!"

I laughed and wrapped my arm around her shoulders. Then we went off looking for the party.

The closest thing we found was a bunch of folks getting high on the front steps to the main dorm. It hit me right in the nostalgia bone.

The joint was passed, and we all talked about the various activities happening over the weekend and the friends we were disappointed didn't show.

Ashley hit it off with a guy we had only sort of hung out with back in college—Maxwell. At one point I told the group I was heading to bed.

"In that back of that gross-ass rented SUV?" Ashley asked.

"That was the plan."

"Girl you are so white trash."

I nodded. It was a sweetly familiar pattern between the two of us. I'd call her bougie, she'd call me white trash, and we'd both love it.

"You're sleeping in my room tonight," Ashley said.

"Are you sure?" I said with a casual tone, though my eyes were clearly saying, *"Are you suuuure?"*

To hide my actual question, I was grateful for the night,

the general cluelessness of boys faced with women's subtext, and the fact that Maxwell was legally blind.

"I'm sure," Ashley said, implying the 'chicks before dicks' part of her answer with her own eyebrow waggles.

I unrolled my sleeping bag on the floor of the dorm room. I was just drifting off when Maxwell and Ashley stumbled in. Their awkward single bed fumbling gave me another bite of nostalgia. I used to lie awake in many a dorm-room bed, listening to my roommate and friend, imagining what stage of coitus they were engaged in based on nothing but the moist sounds they made. I'm pretty sure Ashley and Maxwell got to third base that night.

The next day Ashely made it perfectly clear she was sex-iling me from her own room that night. I had no problem with this.

It was also my last night at the reunion, when we were destined to become the drunk assholes we had feared when we watched the old reunioning revelers a mere five years prior.

Dancing happened. Drinking also happened. The party moved from the on-campus discotheque to the lobby of the dorm. Despite the full lights and dwindling booze supply, we did our young selves proud.

I found some girls who had friend-dopted me when I was friend-dumped my senior year. I loved these girls. They were powerhouses—the kind that could go on a weekend-long bender, then run three miles on Monday morning to sweat out the booze, and ace a chemistry test an hour later. Unfortunately for me, they were all straight. So while I wanted to jump their bones in college, I never got the chance.

However, regret and adulthood were powerful aphrodisiacs. Rebecca was my biggest crush of them all—a six-foot-tall, blond rugby star who had a penchant for drunkenly boxing with friends on the front lawns of parties, and who got more charming the more sloppy drunk she got. And that night, we were all sloppy drunk.

We ended up cuddling on the couch while everyone danced in various states of costumery or undress. I said I regretted the fact that she was straight, which she rebutted with a delightfully too-loud, "I'm not THAT straight!"

"How not straight?" I slurred.

"This not straight," she said, and planted a wet kiss on my lips. She pulled back and giggled, her face pink and her eyes nearly hidden by her apple cheeks.

"Rad," I said, then pulled her into another kiss.

It was that kind of night, or perhaps that kind of group of old friends, where two drunk-ass girls making out on a couch in broad fluorescent light made everyone just go "Awww!" and "Yippie!" and high-five each other just to have someone to high five.

Eventually we stumbled out of the dorm and into the small lot where my SUV was parked.

We climbed in the back.

We had the sex.

It was fun in that drunken, fumbling-in-the-back-of-an-SUV kind of way. Rebecca had a bottle of water she kept forcing me to drink from. God, I loved that girl. Her ability to get wasted and keep her head about her was one of her greatest talents.

After she came for a third or fourth time, she started to cry and confessed that she had a boyfriend who was currently in rehab.

"Would this be cheating?" I asked.

"Yeah, I think so," she said.

"Is that something you're okay with dealing with?"

She sniffed her tears. "Yeah. It is."

We slept the sleep of the wicked and the drunk.

The next morning I felt shockingly together, though I saw the shame on Rebecca's face. I kissed her cheek and said I had a wonderful time and was there anything she needed to say or do to feel okay? She shook her head, and I could see that she'd have to sweat this out of her system, too.

I took a quick look around the lot to make sure no one was around then opened the back of the SUV so we could spill out. Rebecca did her small walk of shame back to the dorm, and I did mine to the bathroom to clean myself up.

At the bridal shower restaurant, I was greeted with warm welcomes from my family. My headache throbbed in time with the soft jazz coming from the speakers. Only my mother noticed that I looked "a little rough." Everyone else was too dazzled by the fact that I was wearing a dress to notice the bags under my eyes. My mom handed me a full-to-the-brim champagne flute and told me to go hug my grandmother.

After making the rounds, I found my sister, radiant in a yellow dress. "How was your night?" she said with a knowing grin.

"I had sex in the back of the SUV with a girl I've been crushing on for the past seven years. I got maybe 2 hours of sleep. And I'm not sure I washed my hands well enough to be touching all of our relatives."

"Sounds like you. Here," she said refilling my glass with

champagne. "Hair of the dog."

"Thanks," I said before gulping it down.

"You're welcome. Now go wash your hands before we do the cake."

strange bedfellows

As an author, I hit up a handful of writing conferences each year. My favorite of all of them is a feminist science fiction and fantasy conference. It packs a double whammy of people and ideas that get me going cerebrally and genitally. Big time turn-ons all around. You may be familiar with the term "sapiosexual." Smart people make me wet.

The conference attracts feminists, queers, scholars, fans, authors, illustrators, gamers, geeky polymaths, and more. The problem is that, while each of these kinds of people may be easy enough to hit on by themselves, when you combine them all into one big group, it creates a sea a mile wide of hot, smart, sexiness, and a mile deep of abject awkwardness.

I am one of those awkward people. I can't read signals. I never assume women find me attractive. I write books mainly to have an excuse to avoid going out in public. Most people don't believe that because I'm fairly charming and outgoing, but if you get me one on one and try to sleep with me, it's going to be deeply uncomfortable for both of us.

It's not that I'm cold or aloof. I'm just super weird most of the time.

The first year at this conference, I didn't even get close to getting laid. I had a million crushes, but no one made a move and so we all just got our freak on in more table-top gaming sorts of ways.

The next year I resolved to remedy the situation. After all, in the land of the awkward, the *slightly less* awkward person is queen.

I resolved to be the least-awkward queen of the feminist sci-fi con. The first part of my plan was to be in front of as many people as possible. This was easy. I like being on panels and reading and generally performing. This would be my opportunity to be my shiny self and hope that it was enough.

The second part of the plan was to, after speaking in front of a large group of people, stand quietly in the corner and hope that one or two sexy people would be interested enough to try to get into my pants.

There was no third part of the plan. Slightly less awkward was all I aimed for. This was going to have to do.

The first of three nights at the conference, I was on one late-night panel about sex and fantasy fiction. I waxed poetic about fucking and shapeshifting for an hour, and then I stood in the corner to begin phase two.

A cute, skinny, blonde girl approached. Mollie. She was the nanny at the con during the day so she could only socialize in the evenings. She chatted me up and it was clear there was some sexy potential afoot.

The second night I was hitting up all the parties in the

hotel and getting into various science-fiction themed shenanigans. I drank green booze out of test tubes, ate liquid nitrogen-made ice cream, and got into an argument about why Gandalf didn't just have the eagles take the ring to Mount Doom.

At the SF/F Writers of Color party, my awkward returned. Everyone at the party was so sexy and smart, I felt all the mojo I cultivated seeping away. I drank my test tube alone in the hallway, pretending to read my texts. My terrible cover was interrupted by Mollie. She bouned over to me and slathered on the charm. I felt terrible, knowing that I just didn't have the nerve to do what she wanted me to do, which was shove my tongue down her throat, or at least invite her back to my room.

When my awkward barrier didn't crack despite her hardcore flirting, she gave me the line. You know the line:

"I've never been with a girl before."

Now, I know that's supposed to be the bicurious mating call. "Ca-caw! I've never been with a girl before! Ca-caw!"

To me, that line is lady-boner kryptonite. As someone who's dated girls since I was in high school, sleeping with bicurious women really loses its appeal after a while. Fucking virgins just isn't my kink.

This is for a few reasons. First, it assumes that virginity is a real thing that can be given or taken, as opposed to a concept invented by men to make them feel special for sticking their dicks in something for the first time. Second, if we do fuck, the bicurious girl is either going to be totally aroused or totally disgusted by my genitals, and I don't know which it's going to be until we're naked. Third, if she's into it, it can get deeply problematic with the gender-fetishizing language. "Oh my gosh," she might say, "You smell so good. You're so soft!"

I know these are nice things on the surface, but the underlying context is that these comments come from being compared to men. As in, "You smell so good because you don't smell like ball sweat!" "You're so soft because you don't have a thousand tiny daggers attached to your face that will spear my delicate thigh flesh when you go down on me."

These aren't true compliments, only poorly veiled critiques of male grooming habits.

Finally, if we do end up having sex, it means that I'm probably going to have to do all the work. The work is, mind you, not just proving that I'm good in bed, but rather proving that lesbians as a group can hold their own when sleeping with women who only sleep with men.

Honestly, sometimes I'm not in the mood.

But then again, it was the second night of a three night con. So…

I stood there awkwardly, giving her zero ground.

Finally, she laid down her trump card. "Listen," she said, "I'm going to go to bed. I have to wake up early to work."

This is when any normal, not awkward person would say, "Hey, c'mere," and then shove their tongue down her throat.

But the awkward was strong with me, so I said goodnight and let her walk down the hallway.

I kicked myself for being such a dork, then a fan-type person started chatting me up. As a writer, this is a close second to getting laid. If I can't hear how hot my pussy is, I'll gladly listen to how you like my books.

Half-way into this person's theories about bipedal versus quadrupedal werewolves, I heard from down the hall, "Oh fuck it!"

I turned to see Mollie running toward me. She grabbed my face, shoved me against the wall, rammed her tongue down my throat, and literally threw herself on me. Which is a signal I can read.

In one drunkenly graceful move, Mollie grabbed my hand, dragged me down the hall and into her room, and threw me onto the bed. Somehow I ended up naked. I'm not sure how this happened.

I stared at the hotel room ceiling and it occurred to me that she may have been lying. Because Mollie ate me out like a fucking pro. She ate me out like a Dykes on Bikes benefit picnic.

I'm not sure if her ex-boyfriend had a tiny penis that resembled a clit or what, but she performed authoritatively and gracefully.

She ate me out and I came hard. Then she hand fucked me, and I came again. At this point I had two orgasms by a girl who'd "never been with girls before."

You know what, kid? I thought in my drunken, post-orgasmic bliss. *You've got a bright future.*

Mollie cuddled against my chest and said, "I should probably get some sleep. I have to wake up early."

She didn't even want reciprocation! She just wanted to *do* me. If all bicurious girls were like that, I might have to reexamine my stance.

In my stupor I felt around for my clothes. I sat up on my elbow and found my bra, draped over the side of a crib. Then

I glanced around and saw that the entire room was tiled with baby cribs. The only clear floor was the path we took from the door to the bed. The rest of the room was cribs.

Luckily they were empty. But it was still a bit of a buzz kill. It took me a second before I remembered she was the nanny, so she needed me out of the room so that the parents could drop off their kids in the morning.

I put on my bra while warily eyeing the sheer number of babies these cribs could house.

Mollie caught me looking, leaned close to my face and whispered, "I've got so many babies."

I assembled my clothes and realized, if there's one thing that can trump awkward, it's fucking wacky.

bad dyke

Sometime in college, I discovered I had a penchant for bi-sexual boys.

At first I didn't know what I was doing. My freshman year, I dated two men at once, two friends, Dan and Eric. It didn't feel like cheating, though classically speaking it was. After I told Dan that I had slept with Eric, and he was generally cool with it, it felt like something else was possible. Like we could all be together, maybe.

I had no models for this. I just knew that it felt right and everyone seemed generally okay with the situation.

That relationship ended when Dan moved abruptly back to Los Angeles, and I was left confused, heartbroken, and eighteen. Without him, my relationship with Eric faded into a casual friendship.

But I was left with an understanding that what I wanted, however ill-defined, was possible.

It being college, there was no shortage of confused men running around. Most of the ones who liked me were on their way to gay but making one last play for pussy. Boys like that dug me because I didn't shame them for wanting dick, or doing drag, or lacking girl-part experience. I liked them right there, on that cusp of figuring everything out. The moment before clarity is always my favorite.

I finally had the boy-boy-girl threesome I itched for on my nineteenth birthday. It imploded, uninterestingly, as such things often do, as soon as the genitals came out. The threesome had been preceded by a wild party that featured a drunk stripper who rubbed his sweaty sack all over my face in front of my friends. If my sexuality were constructed by a series of tick marks in columns marked "men," "women," and "other," that moment would have placed at least three points in the "women" column.

Once I moved to Los Angeles, I started buying into the myth that there were no male bisexuals. Though I clearly knew and loved many of them, every man I met in Los Angeles (with the possible exception of a few actors on my TV show—fingers crossed) was firmly on one of the two "Pussy yay" or "Pussy nay" teams. None of the men I knew were even willing to entertain the possibility of flexibility, sensuality, or open-heartedness. They firmly policed their masculinities—gay or straight—often assisted by the women who knew them. It all helped further alienate in my own mercurial attractions.

Two years into my time in Los Angeles, I was playing exclusively on the "Pussy yay" team. My transition to full-time lesbo was completed by taking a job at the Los Angeles Gay & Lesbian Center in the Cultural Arts Department. I wasn't just a lesbian, I was a *professional* lesbian.

One morning, a few weeks after the easiest breakup of my life, I got word from my boss that I'd need to babysit a bunch of obnoxious New Yorkers who were renting the Center for the weekend. I grabbed my laptop and sunglasses and prepared for a shitty Sunday.

In the courtyard of the building, I introduced myself to the people who mattered, then I camped out at a patio table to work on whatever play I was writing at the moment. When I went to get coffee, I was shortstopped by a big blond man in a pink shirt.

"Hi!" he said. "You work here?"

"Yes. Do you need anything?"

"Nope." He shrugged. "Just wanted to thank you for helping out today. My name's Reid."

"Okay."

"Do you want a cocktail?"

"It's eleven a.m."

"Brunch time! We have a mixer sponsor. Do you want tangerine or cranberry?"

I looked around the courtyard as though my boss would peer out from behind a tree, scolding. "Tangerine," I mumbled.

"Do you want to sit with me? My boyfriend is on panels all day."

I retrieved my laptop and joined Reid at the deserted info table. He asked about the work we did at the Center, and I launched into the boilerplate about our homeless youth program, AIDS services, senior program, and more.

"And the art?" he asked referencing the gallery behind us.

"I curate it."

"Wow."

He asked about our AIDS health services, which segued into how HIV impacted the arts in the 80s and 90s. He talked about the closet and bi-invisibility, especially for men, which segued into the New York sex party scene.

He asked me about my own sexual identity.

"Lesbian," I said. "You?"

"Bi," he said. "And poly."

"What?"

"Non-monogamous. My boyfriend and I are in an open relationship. I love men, but I prefer dating women. Queer women if I had to put a fine point on it."

There was a lull while I looked at him as though a tentacle emerged from his forehead and started conducting a symphony. "You date lesbians?"

"If they'll date me."

"How does that even work?"

He smiled and took a sip of his mimosa, pinky aloft. "Quite well, actually."

I wanted to scold him, to reiterate the definition of "lesbian" for him as though he were another douchebag who didn't understand what a no-man zone meant. But it didn't sound as though he was coercing anyone. I realized after my initial shock that it wasn't that I thought he was a creep. It was that I didn't believe him. How could I? I had never met a man who preferred queer women—I mean *real* queer women. Plenty of straight guys joked that they were lesbians trapped in a man's body, but it was always clear that these men got their cultural cues about lesbians exclusively from porn. They usually ate pussy like "lesbians" in porn, too.

But this was a guy who insisted he dug flannel-wearing, mullet-having, pussy-eating, diesel dykes.

"Really?"

"I like women who don't need me. Who don't need men at all. I guess it makes me feel special to be one of the only dudes a woman wants. But mostly I like women who are comfortable in their own skin. Who don't need to wear high heels or makeup just to feel pretty. Women who like getting their hands dirty. Utilitarian. Sporty."

"Lesbians," I said.

"Lesbians," he repeated.

I sat back in my chair and took another sip of my tangerine thingy.

"But doesn't that screw up their identity? Sleeping with dudes?"

Reid reached forward to grasp my knee, but paused, his big hand hovering over my leg.

"I realize I want to touch you to emphasize what I'm about to say, but I don't want to touch you without your permission."

The moment held a gravity for me I couldn't have anticipated. I believe it was the first time in my entire life anyone, especially a man, had asked before touching me. I would have laughed if the depth of that realization hadn't horrified me.

Reid held still. I smiled. "Go ahead."

He squeezed my knee in a casual, friendly gesture. "Anyone I date, or sleep with, or love. Their identities are their own, influenced by far more important things than my dick. I mean, my dick is important," he laughed. "But not enough to take away anyone's identity or community. You are who you say you are. Other people's opinions are irrelevant."

I took a heavy breath as his point lingered in my head. He

removed his hand.

Another hour of animated conversation passed. Reid's boyfriend, an equally linebacker-sized black man with a big voice and animated presence, joined us briefly, then returned to the theater.

"So," Reid said, after a small lull in the eager stream of talk. "I have a question for you. But I don't want to freak you out."

"Okay," I said warily.

"Do you want to go make out?"

The word "No" was cued up in my brain, as it always was when I talked to men about pretty much anything. A lifetime of experience taught me that it was better to have that word prepared than risk needing it and not having it at the ready.

But I didn't say "No."

I didn't say anything. I thought about my ex, and how our sex life had been fine, but meager. I thought back to the last time I had sex before her, and how long it had been. I thought about how many years had passed since I had kissed a man, and how I had actually liked it when I did. I looked at Reid. He grinned sweetly.

"Yeah," I said. "Okay."

The Center had a hallway that employees affectionately referred to as "Hookup Alley." It's like Diagon Alley but with different kinds of wands. Hookup Alley was a fire exit with doors that didn't lock. There were no cameras, and it was rarely used except by men after their AA meetings who wanted to engage in a little sober entertainment.

I had forgotten the keys to my office, so I took Reid there. What ensued was likely the only hetero-paired make out session ever seen in Hookup Alley. And also the hottest. The hottest and the only.

Yes, it was strange. And yes, I was still a lesbian as far as I was concerned. But it was hot and hit the spot, and I was happy that I said yes.

We reassembled ourselves and went back to the courtyard to wrap up the event. Reid invited me over to his boyfriend's place in Mid-City for lunch the next day.

His boyfriend wasn't thrilled to see me at his condo, but Reid was delighted. He made tuna salad and offered me a back rub.

We cuddled in a sunbeam like two puppies, and he invited me to stay on after his boyfriend left so we could have sex. Between the vibe from the cranky boyfriend and my still solid lesbian identity, I declined.

Since I had come out for the third time as a lesbian, my experience in the community had thrived. I had found lovers and friends, and I felt an ease in my own body I'd never experienced before. Even casual sex had become something more honest and sweet. I wasn't ready to give it up because of a hot make out session with a dude. Though I had certainly liked, lusted after, and loved men in my past, I wasn't ready to turn my back on an identity that had given me so much.

Instead of fucking the dude, I went on a bike ride.

I was training for the AIDS LifeCycle, a 565 mile bike ride from San Francisco to Los Angeles, which to me meant smoking a joint in Playa Del Rey and biking up the boardwalk to grab a burger. The burger joint was empty but for a group of three men.

I ordered a beer and a burger and cracked open *Big Sur*

and the Oranges of Hieronymus Bosch, which I had picked up at the Henry Miller Library on my last trip down the PCH from San Francisco.

It was hard to focus on the book. One of the three men was bragging, drunkenly and loudly, about getting his "cunt of a boss" fired. The story was a string of misogynistic invective, goaded by his cronies. Every detail was colored by his hatred of working for a woman, occasionally spiced up with anti-Chicana racism. I couldn't focus on anything but the bullshit these men spewed.

Praying for them not to notice me, I drank quickly and read and reread the lines on the page. Every bit of my righteous feminist and lesbian rage bubbled at the top of my consciousness. The part of me that wasn't praying for invisibility was begging for the chance to skewer them.

Eventually the ringleader did notice me. On his way back from the bar with a fresh round for his meatheads, he asked me what I was reading. "Henry Miller" I muttered, giving him the sharpest eye-daggers I could muster.

He proved my hypothesis. He was such a moron he didn't even realize what kind of conversational opening I gave him by invoking the name Henry Miller.

He said something too dumb to remember and returned to being a hero to his repugnant friends.

I watched them pal around, laughing at those who they thought were inferior to their masculinity, their whiteness, their entitlement. And I realized, book in lap and beer in belly, that I was putting Reid in the same group as them. I was telling myself I couldn't let myself like him, because he was a man, and men were like these guys: oafish, bigoted, small-minded.

But Reid wasn't any of those things. He was bright and compassionate and big-hearted. I had been tamping down my budding feelings for him because his Y-chromosome represented all of the things I was trying to escape in this world, all of the horrible things represented by masculinity. It was as though by divesting myself from men, I could render myself immune to, or at least apart from, the patriarchy. In doing so, I was ignoring the beauty and nuance that masculinity could hold. It was fair to neither Reid nor me to lump him into this douchebag triumvirate.

On the slightly stoned, slightly drunk bike ride home, I realized that there was more to him, to me, to all of it, than I had given myself permission to explore. And that to turn down the possibility of love, or at least connection, because it came in a package I didn't think I was supposed to like, was myopic and ungrateful. Instead, I chose gratitude and an open mind. It paid off in ways I wasn't anticipating. And it gave me a new appreciation for the possibilities and permutations of my own relationship with the world.

Two years later when I left my job at the Center, I walked past where Reid and I had leaned against the wall in Hookup Alley, and I saw a hand print, faint as anything, but clearly there. A perfect print of Reid's hand, just above where my head had been, bracing himself as we started something brand new.

porn star hash

When my partner Reid and I were first getting together, he lived in New York and I lived in LA. When he visited me, he would stay for a few weeks at a time. I lived in an apartment that I still think of fondly. It was the top floor of this prewar building in Hollywood. I called it the Penthouse. My door opened up onto the roof, and I had a 360 degree view of Los Angeles. My writing nook overlooked the Hollywood sign and Griffith Park. The window over my kitchen sink overlooked Paramount Studios, Beverly Hills, and on a clear day, you could see the ocean. That happened twice in five years, but you theoretically could see all the way to the ocean.

Reid and I had an open relationship from the beginning. We had sex for the first time in a five-some. It was love at first strap-on. And though we had other lovers and it was all on the up-and-up, in the first few months of our relationship we were in heavy New Relationship Energy mode, which meant we were spending a lot of focused one-on-one time with each other, and we weren't having a lot of sex with other people.

One morning during one of Reid's visits, I'm getting ready to go to work, and Reid says, "Hey it's my friend's birthday today, so I was going to invite her over and give her a, y'know, special 'birthday present.' Would that be okay?"

"Sure," I say. "Just so you know, though, I'm only working a half day, so when I come home you two might still be... doing it."

"That's great!" he says. "She'd love to meet you!"

"Okay, great! I would love to meet her!"

As I leave the apartment, I pat myself on the back and think, *Our first negotiation! We are excellent at non-monogamy!*

I go to work. I come home.

As I'm walking up the stairs, I hear some sounds. Sex sounds. And talking sounds. In fact, it's ardent sex and moaning followed by energetic, lucid conversation, and then back to ardent sex moans, and back to lucid conversation. I stand at the door, key in hand, waiting for the ardent conversation. On the first cogent phrase I hear, I unlock the door and head in.

I see Reid, my new lover, face down, buried in the pussy of Nina Hartley, the most famous porn star in America.

For a split second I feel like William H. Macy in *Boogie Nights*, except for the whole murder/suicide thing.

Nina Hartley, thoroughly naked, looks up at me, waves, and says, "Oh you must be Allison! It is so nice to meet you!"

Reid springs up, covered in sweat and with Nina Hartley all over his face. His sex hair is all crazy. He bounds over to me like a 250-pound golden retriever, his metaphysical tail wagging. "Welcome home! I love you! Do you want to smoke some hash?!"

Now, for those of you who are contemplating opening up

your relationship, I suggest the best possible things to say when your partner comes home to find you fucking someone else are:

1) Welcome home!

2) I love you!

3) Do you want to smoke some hash?

Trust me, I'm a sex and relationship educator. Just put that one in your back pocket for a rainy day.

Because I'm not a moron, I say, "Yes, yes I would like to smoke some hash."

Reid and Nina lead me into my kitchen, both buck-naked. Feeling a little over dressed, I strip down to my bra and underwear.

On my kitchen table, Nina has set up a rig. It's a pin/button thing like you'd wear on a denim jacket, resting on the flat end with the pin sticking up straight. On the end of the pin is a ball of hash. Overtop the whole thing is a wineglass. Nina demonstrates how to light the hash until it smolders, place the wine glass over it all, let the bell of the glass fill with smoke, then slide it to the edge of the table, where you lean down and inhale the now cool and delicious smoke.

This is technology I have never seen before. I'm delighted. And before long, I'm super-duper high.

Thus, I proceed to stand nearly-naked in my kitchen with the most famous porn star in America and my new lover, getting totally lit on Porn Star Hash.

This relationship has a future, I think.

Nina and I start chatting, and I ask her a question I love asking new friends, which is "What's the most picturesque sex you've ever had?"

I like this question because it doesn't have to be good sex. It doesn't even have to be sex with someone you like. It just has to be pretty. We've all had pretty sex, even if it was terrible in every other way.

Reid tells a story about a castle in Tuscany with olive oil covered bodies that is both hot and gustatorially stimulating.

I tell a story about sex on a balcony overlooking the Pyrenees. The sex was mediocre in every way, but the view was stunning.

Then Nina tells her story. She gets a wistful look on her face. It is so obvious in this moment that for Nina sex is her ultimate expression of self. She tells a detailed story of a night fifteen year prior, in a villa. The light of the full moon streamed through the open window and illuminated her partner's perfect cock. She was so overwhelmed by the beauty she knelt before him and worshipped his cock.

It's at this point I need to raise my hand. "Pause!" I say. "I was a lesbian until about three months ago when I met this guy, and I spent most of my time trying to keep dick away from my face. So I'm not familiar with this 'cock worship' of which you speak. What is it?"

Little did I know that question, "What is ______?" is the Nina Hartley genie-in-a-bottle phrase.

Nina isn't just a porn performer, she's an educator. Her mission in life is to spread the gospel of great sex through as much of the media as she can. So when I ask, "What is cock worship?" she wordlessly takes my hand, grabs a glass of water, and leads me into my living room. Over her shoulder she calls, "Reid, dear, would you mind lending us your cock?"

Because Reid is not a moron, he follows.

Nina lays Reid down on the living room floor and kneels in front of him with the glass of water. She proceeds to teach me about fellatio.

Because she's a consummate educator, she explains penis anatomy, which I'm not that familiar with, and draws analogues with vulvas, which I'm super familiar with.

"So you know how you can tug on the inner labia and it doesn't hurt? It can feel good? That's like scrotal tissue," she says. "And you know how you can put pressure on the internal clitoral structure to generate pleasure? You want to do that to the inner root of the penis."

Prior to this, I had liked penis enough when it was attached to a person I liked, but I never cared all that much about the nuance of them. Now, though, kneeling next to Nina and watching her work her magic, I said, "Teach me *everything*."

She's doing the whole strokey-stroke and the licky-lick and the jerky-jerk. The sun sets and fills the whole room with brilliant orange light.

Nina sits up and says, "Would you like to try?"

Sure, Nina Hartley, I think. *I'll give my boyfriend a blow job in front of you. That's exactly what I want to do right now.*

I kneel in front of Reid, open my mouth, and lean over. I hear a knock at the door.

Let me remind you. I live on the top floor of a five-story walk up. No one ever knocks on my door. I don't get trick-or-treaters. I don't get UPS guys. It's hard to even get the super over to fix anything. So when there's a knock, I am startled.

I creep to the door, leaving the chain intact, and ease the door open a few inches. Standing on my landing is a girl. She is maybe eleven or twelve.

Plumes of pot smoke rush out the door. Nina Hartley is sucking on cock just outside the girl's range of vision. I wedge myself in the small opening of the door and think, *This is how Allison goes to jail.*

It'll be a story you tell your friends about that slutty moron who corrupted a minor by sheer stupid luck.

The girl rushes ahead with her pitch. "I'm collecting signatures for Youth Leaders in Obama's America. If I get enough signatures, I get to go on a free trip to Washington, D.C., to meet the Obamas."

"That's great," I say. "But I can't help you right now."

"No! It's a program for underprivileged urban youth interested in science and engineering! All you need to do is sign, and I'll get leadership training and a college scholarship, and I'll get to have dinner at the White House!"

This is a good thing, I tell myself. *Don't fuck this up for this sweet, smart girl because your apartment is full of hash and porn stars.*

"Okay," I say, glancing at my half naked body wedged in the door frame. "Do you have a pen?"

She hands me a pen, and I crane my arm down to sign her sheet.

"Great!" I shout, handing the pen back to her. "Say 'hi' to Malia for me!" I slam the door and lock it.

By now the moon is rising over Griffith Park. Reid is lying on his back, stoned and blissful. Nina is leaning over him, tracing her hands up and down his torso.

I kneel next to them, and Nina hands me his cock, saying, "Would you like to suck him together?"

Yes, most famous porn star in the world. Yes I would.

She wraps my hand around the shaft and says, "One thing that's fun when you have one cock and two mouths, is you can kiss through the cock."

That is so romantic.

Nina and I lean in, our mouths on opposite sides of Reid's cock, and we start making out.

My eyes start out closed, but I open them and see Nina's cascade of blonde hair. Beyond Nina's head is my picture window with the full moon rising over Griffith Observatory.

Fuck the Pyrenees, I think.

FUCK THE PYRENEES!

This is the most picturesque sex I've ever had.

foxy & the ridiculous lesbian orgy

WHOEVER FINDS THE *fox, gets to fuck the fox.* These are the words written on the dry erase board of my living room. There are twenty-five half-naked women in my apartment. It is almost two a.m., and the fox hunt is about to begin.

But I'm getting ahead of myself.

When a friend needed an extra "girl-on-girl" story for her live storytelling event, I volunteered immediately. I'd been fucking girls long enough, so I knew there had to be a story in my past somewhere. But a week later, I was wracking my brain for a good story and coming up empty. Well, there was that time when we ran into Baptists while skinny dipping, but it wasn't very sexy. Then there was that epic Scrabble game, but no. I did remember a great story involving my ex and a gnarly yeast infection, but if I told that story on stage I would never get laid again.

I think the problem is that cock is always funny, all the time, but I take pussy very seriously.

I had no story to tell, but the fliers had gone out and time was short. I had no choice. For the sake of science—nay, for the sake of Art, I had to take matters into my own hands. I had to throw a Ridiculous Lesbian Orgy.

Now, I know what you're thinking. If you construct the context for a story, are you actually experiencing the story, or are you just experiencing yourself experiencing the story, thus negating the veracity of the experience? If real things happen in an artificial context, does it count as "true?" I'm a writer, these are the things I think about. Nevertheless, I figured if the story had enough hot dyke action, no one would really care if I pulled a bit of a James Frey up on stage.

I've never read *The Secret,* but living in Northern California, you tend to absorb it from your surroundings. I think the gist is that you send a powerful request out into the universe, and the universe provides.

Well, I emailed out the invitation to the Ridiculous Lesbian Orgy, and not three minutes later I hear from downstairs, "Hey Allie?"

It's my roommate, Lydia. "Hey, Allie? My mom's visiting this weekend. It's cool that she stays here, right?"

My brain screams, "NO! No it's not okay! I'm throwing a Ridiculous Lesbian Orgy! Your mom can't be here!" But then I hear a mild, new-agey voice in my head saying, "Allison, you called this into being. You can't just send it away."

So instead, I say, "Sure, Lydia, that's okay. No, in fact, I *insist* your mother stay here this weekend."

I sent out the invitation on a Tuesday. On Friday night, my apartment is filled with twenty-five half-naked women, and already I consider this a success.

The ridiculous starts right away. We have Hitachi

races, if you know what I mean. And we have Hitachi Jeopardy, which is very, very difficult. Try conjugating French verbs next time you're having an orgasm. Seriously, just try it.

If you've been to an orgy or play party before, you know that there tends to be waves of excitement. There's the first fuck-hungry hump-fest that happens early in the evening when everyone's nervous and excited. Then it kind of mellows out and everyone ends up snarfing at the snack table or processing in the bathtub for a while. The next wave happens rather late, when everyone is finally asking for what they *really* want and fucking who they *really* want to.

Freshly bathed and full of hummus, we're approaching the second wave when my friend decides that she wants a scene of a fox hunt. It's the night before the royal wedding, and everyone's feeling kind of sentimental about Britain, so we say sure, we'll do that.

Foxy congregates seven women and starts explaining the details of a traditional fox hunt in her beautiful (authentic) British accent. The rest of us look warily to one another.

"I didn't sign up for blood play," Dee says.

Foxy assures us that there will be no cutting off of tails and stamping foreheads with bloody stumps. Instead, we'll rip off the bandana she has stuck in the waistband of her underwear, and then we'll fuck her.

And we look to one another and say, "Oh we can totally do that." "Yes, we're in." "Let's go."

She goes on to say we'll each have a role. There's going to be a hunt-mistress and hunters and hound dogs and horses. As she's explaining this, Glo shouts "Wait!" and runs over to her bag and pulls out a bunch of animal hats. There's a bunny rabbit, a panda bear, a tiger, amazingly enough a fox, and there's…a wolf. Now, you should know I have a penchant for wolves, specifically lesbian werewolves, since I spent the past three years of my life writing and publishing two novels about them.

I put on the wolf hat and it seals the deal. I'm in it, finding my inner furry and deciding that she's a pretty rad little wolf. I start to growl and bare my teeth. My fingers curl like paws, and I pull against Tiger's arm as she holds me in place like the good hunter she is. Foxy has us put on strap-ons, so we harness up while we whip ourselves into a frenzy, stretching and jumping, barking and cheering. At this point we're all a little fuck drunk and drunk drunk, so we start going there...fast.

We're blaring trumpets. I'm barking like a big ol' hound dog. We're shouting and making a hell of a ruckus, when we hear a key in the front door.

We are seven women standing in my living room, in bras, panties, huge hard-ons, and animal hats.

And my roommate walks in with her mother.

We stop. We plaster on sweet smiles and call out "Hi!!!" like we're preteens at a slumber party.

Lydia's mom pauses in the living room, takes in the scene, and waves. We wave back. "Okay! Nice to meet you," she says. She hurries to the kitchen, grabs two beers from the fridge, then returns to the guest room and shuts the door behind her.

We launch right back into the trumpet blares and woofing.

We sound the trumpet. Foxy gets a thirty second head start and tears off up the stairs. We hear her heavy footsteps overhead as she tries to find a hiding spot. The footsteps clatter for a bit and then silence.

A thing you should know about my apartment is that it's a rather big loft, but it's not, say, *English countryside* big. So, Foxy gets her head start, but there's not a lot of places to hide.

We charge up the stairs *en masse*, letting the hunt-mistress, Bunny Rabbit, lead the way. She runs to the sitting room and sniffs and waits. Nothing.

Then she leads us to my office. We wait. Nothing.

Then she creeps to the door of my bedroom. We listen, my wolf ears rotating like little satellite dishes. There's an intense pause. Then, with a clatter and an explosion of dirty underwear, Foxy bursts from my hamper. She leaps to my bed to try and escape, but I'm right there and let my newly acquired animal instincts lead the way.

I grab her around the waist and drag her to the floor. She's on top of me, kicking and screaming and biting and punching, but I'm holding tight. The girls are screeching "Flip her over! Flip her over! Flip her over!"

Foxy elbows me in the chest as I flip her over, and I get her ass in the air and her face is buried in my tits. Bunny Rabbit rushes over, grabs the bandana from the back of her underwear, holds it triumphantly above her head, then throws it to the ground. Foxy fights, but she knows she's done for. Bunny Rabbit takes a condom from the top of my bureau and slowly rolls it on her cock.

There's a moment of reverent silence as we all realize, "Oh my. This is a gang bang."

Bunny Rabbit yanks Foxy's underwear down to her knees while I've still got her pinned. She struggles against me, but she's surrendering. Her face is buried so deep in my tits that all I can see of her face is that fox hat. It's staring up at me with these sweet, brown, mendicant eyes. I think, *Oh poor Foxy, you should've run faster.*

Bunny Rabbit lives up to her namesake and gives it to Foxy really good, her ears flopping over her face as she humps like, well, a rabbit. Then Tiger is up with her hot pink harness and dildo, and Foxy groans into my ribcage. Despite the carpet burn I acquired in my wrestling Foxy to the ground, I enjoy the massage on my back as we rock back and forth on a pile of my dirty drawers. By now she's given up fighting completely and is just holding on tight as the women take her in turns.

A procession of be-dildoed women take on the fox, punishing her for her impertinent running and hiding. In the meantime, the rest of the party goers have crept upstairs, sitting on chairs and pillows in a semicircle around my bedroom's open door. One of them is passing around snacks.

Finally, it's Panda Bear's turn. She insists we all call her Mei Sheng. The harness hits her in the right spots, and she's moaning more than Foxy is. From my vantage, all I can see is Foxy's little fox face staring up at me, and cresting over her shoulder there's a little plush panda face staring at me with vacant black eyes. I wonder, is this where Red Pandas come from?

Foxy's near her limit but it's still my turn. I edge out from beneath her and roll a condom onto my fingers to give her a break from all the cock. I ease my fingers into her. She's wet and gaping. As I milk her g-spot whilst all my friends watch through the bedroom's open door, and the moans and shouts of other women echo throughout my loft, I have one singular thought: *The Secret fucking works.*

Talk about declaring something powerfully. *The Secret* is the reason I had twenty-five naked dykes humping in my apartment. It's is the reason I discovered my inner-furry, okay? I'm proud of that. *The Secret* is the reason my besties and I strapped on animal hats and cocks and wailed on our buddy until she couldn't take any more. *The Secret* is the reason I was able to get hella laid after I told the story on stage. And you know what else? I think The Secret can save the world. Seriously. Because I've never met anyone else who could convince a panda to mate in captivity.

howl for me

To people in my kinky, sex-positive community, the simple fact that I had written two novels about lesbian werewolves seemed to indicate some sort of subconscious perversion. People on the street would call out to me, "Hey she-wolf! Awoo!" or I'd get emails from friends addressing me as Wolf Girl.

I found this strange, since all I did was write books about werewolves. This wasn't some weird kink I was foisting on an unsuspecting public. It was fiction. I had to wonder, does JK Rowling get emails from friends saying, "Hey, what's up mudblood?!" Do cops show up at Stephen King's door any time a neighborhood kid gets possessed by a demon?

When I went on tour, it got even weirder. People would ask, "What's your book about?" and when I answered, "Lesbian werewolves" sometimes they would follow up with, "Oh, is it fiction?"

At first I was so stunned by the stupidity of the question, I just answered with a patronizing, "Yeah, duh."

But I got the question enough that I started having fun with it. So when I heard, "Is it fiction?" I would answer, "It's memoir."

Amazingly, some people would continue a line of questioning, and I'd have to expound on my past as a lesbian werewolf.

However, through this playful ruse I learned that if you tell a lie enough times, it can start becoming the truth.

When I arrived home from tour, I found that the fiction within the fiction followed me. I began getting emails from friends asking if the wolf could come out and play.

As a sex geek, getting emails from friends for play dates is nothing new. But getting an email asking not for me, but a subconscious avatar that supposedly lived inside of me, felt sort of odd. Most of my friends are blackbelt kinksters, however, so I had to take it on faith that they saw something in me that I didn't see in myself. I gave them the benefit of the doubt and started saying yes to these invitations. I'd wear a pair of wolf ears and tail to play parties. Then there was the fox hunt orgy, followed by a date with a girl who was into puppy play. In both those scenarios, however, I was playing the wolf as a form of service. Service topping is definitely part of my sexual self-expression, but it's always about the other person's experience. So while I enjoyed test driving the wolf persona (wolfsona?), it didn't inspire any grand epiphanies.

Then I went to Kink Camp.

There are many Kink Camps that go by different names, but most of us enthusiasts refer to all of them by the generic "kink camp." They're like toothpaste in that way.

This specific Kink Camp takes place at an old boy scout camp on the East Coast. It's like Burning Man for kinky perverts. Let me rephrase, it's like Burning Man for *only* kinky perverts. There are glow sticks and e-stim, bonfires and needle play, drum circles and suspension bondage. It's a glorious weekend of folks scening in all sorts of imagination-defying ways. My partner Reid and I were teaching a seminar on open relationships. I usually feel super vanilla compared to the crowd at Kink Camp, but I figured, okay sure, I'll bring my ears and tail, because you never know.

The first day at camp, I wander around wearing my ears and tail. The cool thing about kinky perverts with good protocol is that they ask you permission for everything. So while wandering the grounds, I get a dozen or so people asking me if they could scratch me behind my ears or rub my belly. This is a part of the wolf thing I hadn't anticipated. While I consider myself an introverted misanthrope, I never pass up a head scratch.

I also get invitations to bottom for people. I need to feel a strong heart-connection with someone before I can receive or be submissive. So the easiest answer to all of these sweet folks is "No." But I appreciate the attention nonetheless.

Evening falls over Kink Camp, and Reid says, "Did you know it's a full moon tonight?"

One of my favorite things in the world is outdoor sex. Happily, I found a partner who shares my predilection. We're both queer pagan types, so any opportunity to get all humpty-humpty in the mud is a good one.

We pack a picnic, which in this world includes a duffel bag full of sex toys and our waterproof blanket.

As I'm packing the bag, Reid turns to me and says, "Wear the tail and ears." He's not kinky either, so I'm not sure how to take this. I roll with it, telling myself it's a way to be of service to my beloved.

We walk to a grassy hillside and lay out the blanket. Reid tells me to take off everything, except the tail and ears. "If that's what you want, darling," I say, still pretending that this is all about him. But the way he says it makes it clear that this isn't about him at all. This is something he's going to force me to receive. We've been together many years now, so I trust him with that kind of power, but in the moment it still feels…edgy.

I lay down on the blanket, naked but for the tail and ears. Skyclad, if you will. Reid eats me out vehemently. As I orgasm, the full moon crests the trees at the horizon.

As a squirter, i.e., a woman who ejaculates, I know the feeling of when I want to squirt. It's like there's a roiling in my pelvis, a whirlpool of sexy fluid that's ready to flow. After my first orgasm, I feel it, like there's one in the chamber, waiting for the spark of ignition.

Reid tells me to get on my hands and knees. He gets behind me and fucks me. The combination of the moon and my cycle and kink camp gets my body into one of those places where he can give me as much as he wants and I can just take and take and take it. My cervix shouts, "Party's up here!" and my g-spot is giggling with unabashed delight.

Reid grabs a fistful of my hair and yanks my head back to the sky. He leans over and whispers, "Howl."

When I get really well fucked, I can't verbalize shit, even if is a simple syllable. Instead, I make a series of squeaks.

He yanks my head back again so I'm facing the moon and growls, "Howl!" I continue my indecipherable squeaks and mumbles.

Finally, he grabs me around the chest with his muscled arm, yanks my head back by my hair, and screams, "HOWL!"

"AWOOOOOOOOOOOOOOOOOOOOOO! AW-AW-AWOOOOOOOOOOOOOOOOOOO!!!!"

And I soak everything. Every. Thing. Mama moon was in control.

I lie in a puddle of my own making, spent. The pre-orgasmic division of self and world dissolves into a fuzzy space. My big man holds me as the fragments of my consciousness bleep and bloop back together.

As soon as my liminal brain is back online, I have a thought. During the whole wolf-exploration thing, I was so focused on discovering the wolf, I forgot about the "were" in the werewolf. But werewolves are both. Sometimes they're people. In the world that I created in my books, the werewolves get to choose when they're human and when they're wolves. And lying beneath the full moon, the moonlight reflecting in my puddle of come, I realize that same choice is now mine. I can be either.

I can be both.

all in

I'M NOT AN exhibitionist. I just enjoy having sex in front of large groups of people.

Allow me to explain.

What I love about sex education isn't just giving solid, real information about sex, anatomy, and sexuality, it's also role-modeling for people what's possible. Often this means I use my body and my sexuality to give people permission to explore their own identity and proclivities and to let people know that there doesn't have to be shame and fear associated with the way they like to have sex.

I believe a lot of healing can happen by watching real people have real, connected sex and intimacy. Understanding that humans can enjoy sexuality together in a myriad of ways can help undo a lot of the sexual shame so many of us are brought up with.

I feel like it's a gift I can share by being comfortable with myself. It doesn't mean that I like everything or do everything, god knows. But it does mean that I when I find something I do like, I want to spread the gospel.

In 2007 I'm at Burning Man for the inaugural year of a women's camp called Camp Beaverton. I'm tending camp when a beautiful person with tangerine-colored hair and an impish grin strolls up. They start asking me questions about the camp, and all I can do is wonder where I recognize them from. They ask questions. I answer. Back and forth it goes until an image fills my brain of this person, coming like a firehouse on their lover's face. I realize I'm recalling a scene from a porn called *The Crash Pad.*

I saw this movie as part of Outfest, the LGBT film fest in Los Angeles. If you ever want to see a room full of 200 women squirm, show them a porno starring hot dykes and genderqueers. Lesbians are not used to that whole thing. Porn is one of the places where the "G" of the acronym have the decidedly upper hand.

The person talking to me is one of the stars of the film *The Crash Pad*, and was, in my opinion, the most compelling by a mile. Their name is Jiz Lee, San Francisco's genderqueer porn darling. I do everything I can to maintain my composure as my insides (especially the lower ones) squee with delight.

We hit it off and we end up spending the night together, and it's wonderful. The next day we decide we want to hook up again, so we commandeer my friend's minivan to have a rare, dust-free Burning Man sex experience.

We're having hand sex, and Jiz asks me to add more fingers.

Always happy to accommodate, I upgrade from two fingers (delightful) to three (fantastic). Then they ask for another. I add my fourth finger (smashing). We're fucking like that for a while when Jiz asks me to give them my whole hand.

As a sex educator, I am aware of the mechanics of fisting, but I had yet to do it myself. The whole idea is to make your hand as long and narrow as possible. First, you take your four fingers and squeeze them together as tightly as you can, tucking the pinky to the index finger, making your hand into an arrowhead of love. Then you stretch your thumb across your palm so that it's tucked against the first segments of your two middle fingers. I know these steps. This is as far as I'd ever gotten.

I have my fingers inside of Jiz, and I start putting pressure on the entrance of their vagina. My hand eases in, until I get to the first hardest part.

What's the first hardest part? The lowest knuckles, aka The Widest Part of the Hand.

I add some lube. We take a few deep breaths. I check in with Jiz, and they give me a nod that they're doing great.

I literally press onward.

I get to the second hardest part. What is the second hardest part? It is the base of the thumb. That lowest knuckle is a bear. No matter how tight you tuck, it just doesn't want to flatten out. Bones are a bitch that way.

Nevertheless, we breathe and I ease in. Jiz asks, "Will you make a fist?"

So I tuck my fingers and make a fist. My whole hand is inside Jiz.

And I have the single most profound physical experience of my life. I had never felt so connected during sex as in that moment. I imagine that it feels like what men get to feel, to have such an important part of your body enveloped by your lover's.

It is deep. It is profound. It is beautiful. It is the most intimate thing I have ever felt.

Boys and girls, this is how Allison Moon got hooked on fisting.

A few years later, I move from Los Angeles to Oakland. Jiz and I are still great friends, and they invite me to their 30th birthday party.

I read the invitation and find out it is a live-streamed orgy at the Crash Pad—the venue where they film all their porn.

Now, I had done a lot of performative sex before. I've demo modeled for sex workshops, I've been to orgies, I've done live sex performance, but porn was one of those things I'd never tried. I'd considered it, but I just couldn't ever get there. I love porn and the people who make it. I just had some reservations I couldn't quite reconcile.

But I figured a 30-person orgy would be a great place to pop that cherry. I could disappear into the background and be some sort of "orgy extra" making out at the edge of the screen, slightly out of focus.

I go to the party, and like any porn set, it's a lot of people awkwardly standing around waiting for things to happen.

There are some technical difficulties from the start, so I spend most of my time eating carrot sticks in my underwear.

I'm trying to figure out how I can play. My other friends who are there aren't really feeling the vibe, but I do want to participate in some way. It's Jiz's birthday after all. I want to give them a gift.

Jiz gets the party rolling by giving 30 blow jobs around

the bed. I stand in the doorway watching, and a small freckled trans man named Martin sidles up to me. We start chatting and he's lovely.

Martin asks if I want to play, and I say, "What do you want to do?"

"How would you feel about getting fisted?" he asks.

At this point, I had never taken a fist before. But the dude was tiny. So I say what anyone should say when they're contemplating getting fisted, which is, "Show me your hand."

He holds up his hand in the international symbol for "You can totally take this" which is, again, fingers pulled in tight, thumb tucked across and up.

I'm delighted to find that his hand isn't much girthier than my primary partner's penis.

By this point there are at least fifteen people on the bed with many others surrounding it. We find ourselves a tiny sliver of free bed amongst the throng of writhing bodies. I scootch on the bed and remove my panties. Martin grabs a glove and lube and kneels in front of me. I take a breath and relax. Martin starts warming me up, rubbing my vulva and playing with my clit. It feels delightful.

He gives me one finger and I barely notice it. He adds the second and it feels nice. He adds a third, and it's lovely. He inserts the fourth and, yep, this is sensation. This is what sensation feels like.

I go to my happy place.

Breathe and relax.

I ignore the writhing bodies around me.

Breathe and relax.

I pretend there are no such things as video cameras.

Breathe and relax.

I am on a beach, on a river, sipping a Mai Tai.

Breathe and relaaaaax.

Martin puts pressure against the opening of my vagina with his knuckles. I feel those first four knuckles ease in.

I am on the line of pleasure and terror. Things are… stretching.

Breathe and relax.

This is what the vagina is designed to do. It stretches. Nothing is wrong. It's all part of the plan.

Breathe and relax.

Martin eases his knuckles in, then his thumb. It is *a lot* of sensation.

Breathe and relax.

I'm in my happy place. It's quiet and warm.

Martin moves his hand into a fist. He whispers, "It's in."

I open my eyes and look down at him. His face is flushed. There are beads of sweat at his hairline. He smiles at me. I smile back.

Then I see the camera over his shoulder.

And I remember.

"Oh yeah! WE'RE SHOOTING A PORNO!"

Breathe and relax!

And my pussy is the star of the fucking show.

Breathe and relax!

Allison's vagina, live streaming to your home.

Breathe and relax!

Instead, everything in me clenches.

Martin is now stuck in me like a monkey in a trap. He can't undo his fist or move his hand. He is stuck in me. We are in this together.

We're fine, I tell myself. *This is beautiful. This is educational.*

I look around at the room at all the people having sex. Right next to me on the bed, facing in the opposite direction, is a beautiful woman getting fucked by a hot genderqueer person in a strap-on.

She smiles at me and I smile back. I reach out my hand and she takes it. I turn back to Martin and say, "Let's do this."

Martin starts fucking me with his fist. I feel everything: my cervix, my g-spot, my uterus. Everything is alive. Martin is deeper inside of me than anyone ever had been before.

Fisting is awesome, I think as Martin is wrist-deep in me. *So, so, awesome.*

I close my eyes and indulge in the sensations. My vagina relaxes around Martin's hand and everything starts to feel fantastic.

I open my eyes and grind on Martin. We share a sweet smile. And there's that camera over his shoulder, still trained on my pussy. Hello, America.

Then I turn my head to the right and see *another* camera. This one is focused on my face. The only two cameras for the whole orgy are now all up in my business.

If I didn't want to be in porn, now is a little late to decide. I try not to get too consumed in the possible consequences, lest Martin lose circulation in his arm.

Instead, I think of the educational possibilities. I believe in the profound expansive experience that can happen when you watch two people have connected sex. What can I do right now that can communicate to those people watching at home in De Moines or wherever that what's happening is good and beautiful and possibly something they might want to try in their own lives?

I try to channel all the feelings I'm having in my groin and move them to my face. I start giggling. I flinch. I smile. I moan. I scream. I cry.

I let my face show every emotion that I possibly can, in hopes that whoever is watching it might understand and relate to this experience, no matter how far away in the world they are geographically or experientially.

After we've all cleaned up and hugged, I'm back in the kitchen in my underwear, eating carrot sticks slightly less awkwardly than before.

One of the cameras roams around asking us to give Jiz some birthday wishes.

I look into the camera and smile. "Jiz," I say. "You were the first person I ever fisted, and it was one of the most profound sexual experiences of my life. And today, at your 30th birthday celebration, I got fisted for the first time. I want to say thank you for sharing with me something so real about yourself and for giving me the opportunity to share something real about myself with the many people here in the room and watching at home. I fucking love you. And I fucking love my job."

piercing gays

I AM AT an orgy in midtown, and I am cranky.

Fellow introverts might recognize the source of my malaise. I'm in New York visiting friends. We spent all day at the gay nude beach, and now there is the orgy. Sometime between day time and dinner time, my thoughts have refocused from plans and restaurants to genocide.

And, like the toddler I can often be, I don't recognize my cranky until it was all encompassing.

I arrived at the orgy thoroughly over the whole affair—not just that specific party, but the notion that humans would choose to spend time together in any way whatsoever.

It's one of those times I feel like the dude from that old *Twilight Zone* episode who locks himself in the vault to read and emerges later to find the whole world has been decimated by an atom bomb. The scene where he emerges gives me a joy I assume more normal humans feel during the heroine's big solo in a Disney movie.

"They're all dead!" I'll shout with glee. "I'm all alone!

With my books!"

The party is distinctly kink-oriented, offering few fuck-on-able surfaces but a wide array of wooden blocks, bondage crosses, and a cage.

I'm a vanilla girl with vanilla needs. My idea of an orgy is a party where you fuck, not flog. To each their own, but there is nothing of my own here.

I sit on the couch, watching my partner canoodle with friends old and new, building a grumble so palpable I feel like I'm generating one of those Charlie Brown over-the-head squiggles with my mind.

I'm making small talk with friends when Fiona approaches. Fiona is a sadist. And like so many excellent tops, she can instantly see my state.

"What do you need, sweetheart?" she asks.

I shrug and grumble something about maybe making my way back uptown alone.

But, while I may consider myself vanilla, I share one key thing with masochists: The more I like a woman, the more she scares me. And the more she scares me, the more I like her.

Fiona scares me. She's not only a sadist, she's a *good* sadist. Composed and regal, kind when it counts and mean when it *really* counts.

She makes me feel simultaneously like a bad puppy and a duchess in her court.

She suggests piercing me.

I want to say, "Ha! No! God no!" But I don't. I furrow my brow. I am surprised by my non-reaction. Fiona says, "I'll go get my gear while you think about it."

The first time I was ever pierced, it was my eighth birthday and I was at Claire's Boutique with my mom. I cried so much after they did the first ear that my mom had to take me out of the mall because I was scaring off other customers. My mom had to basically bully me into going back in for the second ear to avoid looking like the lost member of Wham! for the rest of my life.

I'd seen erotic piercings before, but nothing about them was erotic to me. While I wait for Fiona's return, I chat with my friends, all of whom love piercing.

"It's the best natural high," says Chad.

"Piercing is my favorite thing. It's the most intense form of penetration," says Jane.

I realize that what I need is a paradigm shift, and that will be most easily accomplished by endorphins and novelty.

Fiona returns and I say, "Let's do this."

She guides me to the examination table, one of the few padded surfaces in the space. I lie down and she lays out her gear. There are surgical needles, a bottle of rubbing alcohol, gloves, and a tackle box. The tackle box becomes important later.

We discuss the number of needles and placement. I suggest we start small. We agree on six piercings on my chest and add more if I decide I want it.

Chad strokes me with a bunny fur glove as Fiona disinfects my chest.

She tells me to inhale and exhale, and she pierces the first needle through my skin. I can't watch. I squeeze my eyes shut.

It feels like a bee sting. A sharp heat followed by an

intense warming as my blood rushes to the wound.

"I think what I'd like to do," Fiona says, "is decorate your chest with some charms. How does that sound?"

"Uh…sure?"

I have a needle in my breast that was not medically sanctioned and a sadist leaning over me. I am inclined to say yes to whatever she suggested.

Fiona digs through the tackle box, removing a roll of fishing line and pair of surgical scissors. Then she opens the smaller compartment. It contains a vast array of small plastic trinkets including farm animals, ballerinas, fake jewels, and more.

"I'm feeling piglets," Fiona says. "What do you think?"

"Sure," I slur.

Fiona pierces me five more times, three hypodermic needles embedded in each breast.

She strings filament through the needles while I focus on breathing.

Then she takes each piglet, and with a fresh needle, pokes a hole in their plastic, threads the fishing line through, and ties them off.

Fiona asks if I'd like some pictures. I nod.

She takes out her phone, glances quickly around the room to make sure none of the particularly aggressive dungeon mods are watching, and snaps a few photos.

Chad comes back to stroke me with the bunny fur. I feel drunk though I haven't had a drink. I'm high though I haven't smoked. I am, in two words, fucked up.

She helps me sit upright. The weight of my breasts tugs at the piercings. For the first time, I look at her handiwork.

Six piglets, as pink as my flushed nipples, dangle from the swollen skin on my breasts. She teases them a bit, and I feel the filament rub at the inside of my skin. It's a completely novel, sickening feeling.

I feel woozy.

"You want to wander with these in for a bit?" Fiona asks. "Show them off?"

I shake my head. "I think I'm ready to—not have them—if that's alright."

"Of course, baby," she coos. "Let's get you cleaned up."

She takes the scissors, snipping at each filament and dragging it out of my skin.

A small ruby of blood appears at each piercing except one. The middle puncture on my right breast begins with a ruby and turns into a stream, then a river. Blood drips down my breast and splashes on my thighs.

Fiona is unconcerned. "Looks like I nicked a vein," she says like a knitter who dropped a stitch. "I can clean you up," she says. "*Or* I can drizzle some rubbing alcohol over your chest which will make the blood cascade beautifully down your breasts, so they all look like that one."

"Uh," I say, looking up from the already cascading blood, and I do what any good Tennessee William's heroine does, and swoon.

My head lolls back and Chad catches me. My eyes focus on the wooden-slat ceiling.

"I guess that answers my question," Fiona says. "Here we go."

She soaks a cotton ball with alcohol and dabs it at my wound, wiping the blood away. She presses a bandage against my wound, and I take deep breaths. Chad scratches my head and rubs my shoulder.

"Cool, huh?" he says.

I will say this, my mood changed.

I reassemble my clothes and go out to the sidewalk to smoke. My partner joins me there, tentative, testing my mood.

"How was it?" he asks.

"It was a supposedly interesting thing I never want to do again."

"Sounds about right."

"What now?" he asks.

"We go home," I say, "And we fucking fuck."

7 year itch

My partner and I celebrated our 7th anniversary this year. For queer people, that's like 21. For poly people, it's closer to eleventy billion.

Because our relationship has lasted "so long," we've become some sort of oracles for others to visit with their relationship woes. Through the many conversations I've had with these truth seekers, I've determined that there are three primary factors that keep my relationship with my partner Reid so strong.

First, we are transparent and honest with one another, even when it's hard. We show up and do the work, no matter how confronted or triggered we are, even when it means having to swallow our pride or admit we are wrong.

Second, we support each other in our individual self-expressions, including sexual expression, artistic creation, and entrepreneurship. We celebrate our individual successes and support each other through our challenges.

Third, Reid loves me to fuck him up the ass all the time.

It's those three things combined that create a strong foundation of love and trust.

I have to emphasize, our relationship was not "saved" by pegging. This isn't some screwy Dr. Phil bullshit. Our relationship was *founded* on pegging.

Before I met Reid, I identified fully as a lesbian. I was a card-carrying, velvet blazer-wearing, PBR-drinking, self-haircut-at-home-ing, West Hollywood dyke. Then I met Reid, and I was still a dyke because I really wasn't sure what to make of him. I believe I used the words "Cheese Dick" to describe him at one point.

During our first hours-long conversation—before our first hours-long make out session—we talked about Burning Man and the theme camp he was creating for that year's festivities. I had been to Burning Man only once before and didn't love it. It was hard to meet girls, and it was hard to *be* a girl out there. Both these concerns were dissolved when he explained that the camp he was creating was for only queer women. He was creating it because his lesbian friend requested it, but he wouldn't be camping there. While I hadn't planned on going back to Burning Man after that first year, the idea of twenty-some dusty lesbians in a camp together made me reevaluate my stance.

Reid invited me to join the camp, and I became one of the founding members of Camp Beaverton for Wayward Girls.

My second night at the Burn was the Strap-on-a-thon, a women's-only play party hosted by the Beavers. I was a caddy at the party. This meant I would offer lube, dust off dildos, and hold back hair should it be necessary. It also meant that by the end of the four hour party, I was really fucking horny.

I left the orgy dome to deal with the blue clit situation by seeking out some other Beavers.

On top of a big blue school bus parked next to the dome, I found a new crush, Jacinta, along with Reid and two other women. I explained to them my plight, and they took it upon themselves to help in any way they could. While I was only looking for Jacinta, I've never been one to pass up a deal, and four for the price of one is a pretty good deal. On to the pan-gender dome we went.

Inside the dome, the five of us started getting gropey and smoochy and sexy and lovey. Then one of the girls had feelings and needed to leave. So the four of us got gropey and smoochy and sexy and lovey.

I started fingering Jacinta, which was lovely. Then Reid asked if he could go down on me. I hesitated. "I'm a lesbian," I said, "I'm not sure how I feel about prickly chin hairs all up in my business." But then I thought about my blue clit and considered, a mouth was a mouth was a mouth. So I said yes.

He ate me out from behind as I finger fucked Jacinta, and, okay, yeah, that was working quite nicely.

Then I started going down on Jacinta. Reid asked, "Allison, can I fuck you?"

Fucking A, I groaned in my head. *Of course. A guy can't have sex with three women without wanting his dick to be the center of fucking attention.*

But I was trying to be polite, so I said, "Uh, I dunno."

"I have some gloves if you're concerned," he said.

"What?"

"Gloves." he repeated. "For safer hand sex."

"Wait," I said. "You want to fuck me with *your hands?*"

"Of course! What else would I use?"

My heart exploded into a joyous lesbian song. "Well, just for that," I said. "Fuck yeah."

Reid hand fucked me while I ate out Jacinta, and the third girl made out with all of us. We were having a great time. The sexy continued for a while until Reid said, "Allison, I have a request, but I don't want to insult or upset you."

Here it comes, I thought. *Poor lonely dick not getting attention, needing to own the space.*

"Yeah?" I said.

"Have you ever pegged a guy before?"

If there was a Disney movie about queer sex, my heart would have been singing the heroine's song right then.

Always one to try a new experience, I lied and said, "Yes! Yes I have."

Reid harnessed me up and I started fucking him. It was hot and wonderful. It was a lot like fucking a woman with a strap on, but different, and those differences were exciting and fun.

It was, to make another Disney reference, a whole new world.

After all the sex, the four of us cuddled. *Oh my God,* I thought. *I just fucked this guy like a dyke. He fucked me like a dyke. I just had the best lesbian sex at the lesbian camp with the ONE DUDE.*

Three months and dozens of erotically-charged cross-country Skype sessions later, Reid visited me in LA. I was nervous. I had heard horror stories about women excommunicated from their lesbian communities when they started dating men, and I didn't want that to happen to me and my friends.

While Reid and I had a crazy hot connection, I still wasn't sure I was ready to fall in love with a man. I was a dyke, it was so thoroughly my identity that I didn't know if I could give it up. I didn't want to end up a bad dyke.

More than that, even if I could have gotten used to the idea of dating a man, I wasn't convinced he'd really want to date me. Despite his insistence on liking queer women, I was a dyke with hairy legs and armpits. I liked wearing a strap on and eating pussy. I dressed up for dates by putting on a tie and vest, not heels and a dress. What guy wanted that kind of woman?

My friends and I made plans to go out to Jumbo's Clown Room, my favorite strip club in Los Angeles. I wore my butchest outfit and packed, wearing my harness and dildo underneath my jeans. I was basically challenging Reid to prove that he really liked real dykes.

At the strip club Reid endeared himself to all of my friends, even the most skeptical among them. I was shocked, but the dude was charming.

He ordered us a round while we watched the hot strippers be hot on stage. I couldn't help but notice that while all the lesbians' eyes were on the naked ladies on stage, Reid was spending more time staring at the bulge in my jeans.

After the club, we went home, barely making it to the front door before Reid dropped to his knees, pulled out my cock, and started blowing me. I'm not going to lie: my dick is impressive. But he took it all, throat fucking the hell out of me. He wedged his fingers under the straps of my harness and fingered me as he blew me, syncing the movements of his fingers against my g-spot to the moment the tip of my cock hit the back of his throat. Then he stood up and I pulled out his dick. We gripped our dicks together like one big burrito of hot cock, and jerked each other together like two teenage boys in prep school.

I bent him over the bed, spit in my hand, gave him a reach around, and fucked him.

Then he bent me over the bed, gave me a reach around, and fucked me.

The two of us proceeded to have the queerest sex I'd ever had in my life. For the entire length of his stay. Our little hetero-paired bodies insisted, *We'll make this queer. We'll figure out a way.*

I love pegging, not for the power play, but for the gender and sexual orientation play. I feel so fulfilled when I'm enjoying all the various permutations of my body and sexual identity. This is one of the reasons I don't trust dudes who don't take it up the ass; I want to know that my partners can enjoy the range of their own sexualities, too.

For the first time, I wanted a man because he was a man. A queer, self-expressed, sexually self-possessed man. Reid wanted me queer. He wanted me *me*, fully realized and embracing all the gendered expressions of my heart and body. He loved my hairy armpits, my slouchy style, my shaved head, my penchant for packing. My job, it would turn out, was to offer myself the same love and acceptance of my own gender and identity that he offered me.

Seven years later, Reid and I are still figuring out new ways to queer our sex. Yeah, I'm a bad dyke. But I'm the luckiest bad dyke in the world.

Notes & Acknowledgments

Most of these stories were developed and first performed at Bawdy Storytelling, a superb show that is one of the things that makes San Francisco great. It is a truly sex positive event, a shame-free zone, and a raucous good time. Thanks to founder Dixie De La Tour for giving me a stage for my smut. Learn more about the show at BawdyStorytelling.com

"Piercing Gays" was first performed for Kevin Allison's RISK! Podcast.

"Foxy and the Ridiculous Lesbian Orgy" was first published in print by Cleis Press in the book, *Wild Girls, Wild Nights.*

Thanks to my editor Alyc Helms. And thanks to Tatyana Brown for giving me the idea to transcribe these stories and turn them into this book.

Most of all, thanks to the various pseudonymed and not-so-pseudonymed friends who shared their hearts and/or loins with me so that I have some salacious stories to tell.

Also by Allison:

Lunatic Fringe, Tales of the Pack Book 1
Hungry Ghost, Tales of the Pack Book 2
Girl Sex 101

23619537R00079

Printed in Great Britain
by Amazon